PERT Math Workbook

The Most Effective Exercises and Review PERT Math Questions

By

Elise Baniam & Michael Smith

PERT Math Workbook

Published in the United State of America By

The Math Notion

Email: info@Mathnotion.com

Web: www.MathNotion.com

About the Author

Elise Baniam has been a math instructor for over a decade now. She graduated in Mathematics. Since 2006, Elise has devoted his time to both teaching and developing exceptional math learning materials. As a Math instructor and test prep expert, Elise has worked with thousands of students. She has used the feedback of her students to develop a unique study program that can be used by students to drastically improve their math score fast and effectively.

- **SAT Math Workbook**
- **ACT Math Workbook**
- **ISEE Math Workbooks**
- **SSAT Math Workbooks**
- **many Math Education Workbooks**
- **and some Mathematics books …**

As an experienced Math teacher, Mrs. Baniam employs a variety of formats to help students achieve their goals: she teaches students in large groups, and she provides training materials and textbooks through her website and through Amazon.

You can contact Elise via email at:

Elise@Mathnotion.com

PERT Math Workbook

This authoritative PERT Math Workbook makes learning math simple and fun. This updated PERT Exercises reflects the latest updates to help you achieve the next level of professional achievement.

This prep exercise book and features gives you that edge you need to be successful on PERT Math Exam. The PERT Math Workbook covers:

- Number operations/number sense
- Algebra, functions, and patterns
- Equations and Polynomials
- geometry, probability and statistics

This user-friendly resource includes simple explanations:

- ✓ Review thorough breakdown questions of the PERT math test
- ✓ **2,000+ Realistic PERT Math Practice Questions** with answers
- ✓ The Most Feared Subject Made Easier
- ✓ Detailed subjects review, an extensive subject list to help you build your math knowledge
- ✓ **Two Full-length PERT Practice Tests** with detailed explanations for review and study
- ✓ Help test-taker recognize and pinpoint areas to produce better results in less time
- ✓ PERT Prep Exams to hone your test-taking techniques

Anyone who wants to realize the major subjects and subtle guidelines of PERT Math Test, The PERT Math Workbook offers comprehensive, straightforward instruction.

GET THE ALL-IN-ONE SOLUTION FOR YOUR HIGHEST POSSIBLE PERT MATH SCORE (Including 2 full-length practice tests for realistic prep, content reviews for math test sections).

WWW.MathNotion.com

… So Much More Online!

✓ FREE Math Lessons

✓ More Math Learning Books!

✓ Mathematics Worksheets

✓ Online Math Tutors

For a PDF Version of This Book

Please Visit WWW.MathNotion.com

Contents

Chapter 1:

Whole Numbers

Add and Subtract Integers

Find the sum or difference.

1) $(+168) + (+76) =$

2) $(+65) + (-32) =$

3) $217 - 69 =$

4) $(-203) + 179 =$

5) $(-45) + 501 =$

6) $182 + (-265) =$

7) $(-9) + 20 =$

8) $360 - 200 =$

9) $(-10) - (-38) =$

10) $(-67) + (-96) =$

11) $(-143) - 234 =$

12) $1250 - (-346) =$

13) $3 + (-12) + (-20) + (-17) =$

14) $(-28) + (-19) + 31 + 16 =$

15) $(-7) - 11 + 27 - 19 =$

16) $6 + (-20) + (-35 - 24) =$

17) $(+24) + (+32) + (-47) =$

18) $(-35) + (-26) =$

19) $-12 - 17 - 16 - 23 =$

20) $7 + (-21) =$

21) $107 - 80 - 73 - (-38) =$

22) $(20) - (-8) =$

23) $(3) - (5) - (-14) =$

24) $(20) - (6) - (-20) =$

Multiplication and Division

Calculate.

1) $340 \times 8 =$

2) $180 \times 30 =$

3) $(-3) \times 7 \times (-4) =$

4) $-3 \times (-6) \times (-6) =$

5) $12 \times (-12) =$

6) $30 \times (-6) =$

7) $6 \times (-1) \times 5 =$

8) $(-600) \times (-50) =$

9) $(-10) \times (-10) \times 2 =$

10) $165 \times 5 =$

11) $160 \times 80 =$

12) $312 \div 12 =$

13) $(-2,475) \div 3 =$

14) $(-32) \div (-8) =$

15) $384 \div (-24) =$

16) $4,500 \div 36 =$

17) $(-84) \div 2 =$

18) $9,588 \div 6 =$

19) $900 \div (-25) =$

20) $1,680 \div 2 =$

21) $(-81) \div 3 =$

22) $(-1,000) \div (-10) =$

23) $0 \div 250 =$

24) $(-680) \div 4 =$

25) $7,704 \div 856 =$

26) $(-3,150) \div 5 =$

27) $7,268 \div 2 =$

28) $(-48) \div (-4)$

Absolute Value

Simplify each equation below.

1) $|-30| =$

2) $-10 + |-30| + 28 =$

3) $|-48| - |-20| + 12 =$

4) $|-9 + 5 - 3| + |3 + 3| =$

5) $2|2 - 14| + 10 =$

6) $|-6| + |-20| =$

7) $|-36 + 20| + 10 - 9 =$

8) $|-10| - |-23| - 5 =$

9) $|-20| - |-10| + 3 =$

10) $|20| - 28 + |-10| =$

11) $\frac{4|3-6|}{2} =$

12) $|-20 + 9| =$

13) $|-20| \times |5| + 5 =$

14) $|-6| + |-36| + 9 - 3 =$

15) $|-20| + |-20| - 40 =$

16) $13 + |-34 + 15| + |-10| =$

17) $28 - |-63| + 10 =$

18) $\frac{|120|}{|4|} + 6 =$

19) $|-9 + 12| + |32 - 15| + 6 =$

20) $|-20 + 15| + |-5| + 3 =$

21) $\frac{|-32|}{8} \times |-6| =$

22) $\frac{4|4 \times 6|}{2} \times \frac{|-16|}{4} =$

23) $\frac{|2 \times 6|}{12} \times 6 =$

24) $|-10 + 2| \times \frac{|-3 \times 5|}{3} =$

25) $|-100 + 8| - 5 + 5 =$

26) $|-50 + 40| - 10 =$

Ordering Integers and Numbers

Order each set of integers from least to greatest.

1) $7, -8, -5, -2, 3$ ___, ___, ___, ___, ___, ___

2) $-3, -16, 4, 10, 9$ ___, ___, ___, ___, ___, ___

3) $18, -18, -19, 25, -20$ ___, ___, ___, ___, ___, ___

4) $-9, -35, 15, -7, 42$ ___, ___, ___, ___, ___, ___

5) $47, -52, 28, -55, 34$ ___, ___, ___, ___, ___, ___

6) $88, 36, -29, 67, -44$ ___, ___, ___, ___, ___, ___

Order each set of integers from greatest to least.

7) $12, 18, -10, -12, -4$ ___, ___, ___, ___, ___, ___

8) $29, 36, -14 - 26, 69$ ___, ___, ___, ___, ___, ___

9) $75, -26, -18, 47, -7$ ___, ___, ___, ___, ___, ___

10) $58, 72, -16, -12, 94$ ___, ___, ___, ___, ___, ___

11) $-7, 99, -15, -48, 64$ ___, ___, ___, ___, ___, ___

12) $-80, -45, -40, 18, 29$ ___, ___, ___, ___, ___, ___

Order of Operations

Evaluate each expression.

1) $5 + (4 \times 3) =$

2) $12 - (3 \times 5) =$

3) $(16 \times 3) + 10 =$

4) $(15 - 5) - (6 \times 3) =$

5) $22 + (16 \div 2) =$

6) $(16 \times 5) \div 5 =$

7) $(84 \div 4) \times (-2) =$

8) $(9 \times 5) + (35 - 12) =$

9) $60 + (2 \times 2) + 8 =$

10) $(30 \times 5) \div (2 + 1) =$

11) $(-8) + (10 \times 4) + 13 =$

12) $(7 \times 6) - (32 \div 4) =$

13) $(9 \times 8 \div 3) - (10 + 11) =$

14) $(12 + 8 - 15) \times 6 - 3 =$

15) $(30 - 12 + 40) \times (95 \div 5) =$

16) $22 + \big(20 - (32 \div 2)\big) =$

17) $(6 + 9 - 5 - 8) + (18 \div 2) =$

18) $(85 - 10) + (10 - 15 + 9) =$

19) $(10 \times 2) + (12 \times 5) - 12 =$

20) $12 + 8 - (32 \times 4) + 30 =$

Factoring

Factor, write prime if prime.

1) 12

2) 26

3) 32

4) 48

5) 60

6) 64

7) 35

8) 30

9) 56

10) 75

11) 25

12) 18

13) 49

14) 15

15) 42

16) 124

17) 56

18) 40

19) 75

20) 20

21) 96

22) 27

23) 72

24) 50

25) 24

26) 88

27) 68

28) 124

Great Common Factor (GCF)

Find the GCF of the numbers.

1) 8, 12

2) 48, 32

3) 42, 18

4) 10, 15

5) 18, 24

6) 16, 12

7) 80, 45

8) 100, 75

9) 64, 8

10) 36, 72

11) 93, 62

12) 15, 90

13) 60, 30

14) 36, 28

15) 18, 45

16) 35, 42

17) 12, 20

18) 90, 120, 20

19) 49, 144

20) 16, 28

21) 14, 8, 21

22) 4, 16, 20

23) 14, 49, 7

24) 21, 12

Least Common Multiple (LCM)

Find the LCM of each.

1) 6, 9

2) 30, 24

3) 8, 4, 6

4) 15, 12

5) 30, 5, 40

6) 45, 15

7) 15, 10, 8

8) 3, 4

9) 10, 20, 25

10) 64, 44

11) 24, 36

12) 108, 64

13) 20, 10, 40

14) 12, 20

15) 45, 9, 3

16) 27, 63

17) 42, 12

18) 20, 45

19) 25, 15

20) 14, 32

21) 16, 18

22) 9, 17

23) 32, 18

24) 16, 12

Divisibility Rule

Apply the divisibility rules to find the factors of each number.

1) 12   2, 3, 4, 5, 6, 9, 10   13) 18   2, 3, 4, 5, 6, 9, 10

2) 326   2, 3, 4, 5, 6, 9, 10   14) 405   2, 3, 4, 5, 6, 9, 10

3) 748   2, 3, 4, 5, 6, 9, 10   15) 945   2, 3, 4, 5, 6, 9, 10

4) 81   2, 3, 4, 5, 6, 9, 10   16) 186   2, 3, 4, 5, 6, 9, 10

5) 891   2, 3, 4, 5, 6, 9, 10   17) 640   2, 3, 4, 5, 6, 9, 10

6) 345   2, 3, 4, 5, 6, 9, 10   18) 150   2, 3, 4, 5, 6, 9, 10

7) 75   2, 3, 4, 5, 6, 9, 10   19) 350   2, 3, 4, 5, 6, 9, 10

8) 450   2, 3, 4, 5, 6, 9, 10   20) 4,520   2, 3, 4, 5, 6, 9, 10

9) 1,325   2, 3, 4, 5, 6, 9, 10   21) 990   2, 3, 4, 5, 6, 9, 10

10) 78   2, 3, 4, 5, 6, 9, 10   22) 368   2, 3, 4, 5, 6, 9, 10

11) 772   2, 3, 4, 5, 6, 9, 10   23) 208   2, 3, 4, 5, 6, 9, 10

12) 162   2, 3, 4, 5, 6, 9, 10   24) 500   2, 3, 4, 5, 6, 9, 10

Answer key Chapter 1

Add and Subtract Integers

1) 244	9) 28	17) 9
2) 33	10) −163	18) −61
3) 148	11) 377	19) −68
4) −24	12) 1,596	20) −14
5) 456	13) −46	21) −8
6) −83	14) 0	22) 28
7) 11	15) −10	23) 12
8) 160	16) −73	24) 34

Multiplication and Division

1) 2,720	11) 12,800	21) −27
2) 5,400	12) 26	22) 100
3) 84	13) −825	23) 0
4) −108	14) 4	24) −170
5) −144	15) −16	25) 9
6) −180	16) 125	26) −630
7) −30	17) −42	27) 3,634
8) 30,000	18) 1,598	28) 12
9) 200	19) −36	
10) 825	20) 840	

Absolute Value

1) 30	9) 13	17) −25
2) 48	10) 2	18) 36
3) 40	11) 6	19) 26
4) 13	12) 11	20) 13
5) 34	13) 105	21) 24
6) 26	14) 48	22) 192
7) 17	15) 0	23) 6
8) −18	16) 42	24) 40

25) 92   26) 0

Ordering Integers and Numbers

1) $-8, -5, -2, 3, 7$

2) $-16, -3, 4, 9, 10$

3) $-20, -19, -18, 18, 25$

4) $-35, -9, -7, 15, 42$

5) $-55, -52, 28, 34, 47$

6) $-44, -29, 36, 67, 88$

7) $18, 12, -4, -10, -12$

8) $69, 36, 29, -14, -26$

9) $75, 47, -7, -18, -26$

10) $94, 72, 58, -12, -16$

11) $99, 64, -7, -15, -48$

12) $29, 18, -40, -45, -80$

Order of Operations

1) 17

2) -3

3) 58

4) -8

5) 30

6) 16

7) -42

8) 68

9) 72

10) 50

11) 45

12) 34

13) 3

14) 27

15) 1,102

16) 26

17) 11

18) 79

19) 68

20) -78

Factoring

1) 1,2,3,4,6,12

2) 1,2,13,26

3) 1,2,4,8,16,32

4) 1,2,3,4,6,8,12,16,24,48

5) 1,2,3,4,5,6,10,12,15,20,30,60

6) 1,2,4,8,16,32,64

7) 1,5,7,35

8) 1,2,3,5,6,10,15,30

9) 1,2,4,7,8,14,28,56

10) 1,3,5,15,25,75

11) 1,5,25

12) 1,2,3,6,9,18

13) 1,7,49

14) 1,3,5,15

15) 1,2,3,6,7,14,21,42

16) 1,2,4,31,62,124

17) 1,2,4,7,8,14,28,56

18) 1,2,4,5,8,10,20,40

19) 1,3,5,15,25,75

20) 1,2,4,5,10,20

21) 1,2,3,4,6,8,12,24,32,48,96

22) 1,3,9,27

23) 1,2,3,4,6,8,9,12,18,24,36,72

24) 1,2,5,10,25,50

25) 1,2,3,4,6,8,12,24

26) 1,2,4,8,11,22,44,88

27) 1,2,4,17,34,68

28) 1,2,4,31,62,124

Great Common Factor (GCF)

1) 4

2) 16

3) 6

4) 5

5) 6

6) 4

7) 5

8) 25

9) 8

10) 36

11) 31

12) 15

13) 30

14) 4

15) 9

16) 7

17) 4

18) 10

19) 1

20) 4

21) 1

22) 4

23) 7

24) 3

Least Common Multiple (LCM)

1) 18

2) 120

3) 24

4) 60

5) 120

6) 45

7) 120

8) 12

9) 100

10) 704

11) 72

12) 1,728

13) 40

14) 60

15) 45

16) 189

17) 84

18) 180

19) 75

20) 224

21) 144

22) 153

23) 288

24) 48

Divisibility Rule

1) 12   <u>2</u>, <u>3</u>, <u>4</u>, 5, <u>6</u>, 9, 10

2) 326   <u>2</u>, 3, 4, 5, 6, 9, 10

3) 748   <u>2</u>, 3, <u>4</u>, 5, 6, 9, 10

4) 81   2, <u>3</u>, 4, 5, 6, <u>9</u>, 10

5) 891   2, <u>3</u>, 4, 5, 6, <u>9</u>, 10

6) 345   2, <u>3</u>, 4, <u>5</u>, 6, 9, 10

7) 75   2, <u>3</u>, 4, <u>5</u>, 6, 9, 10

8) 450   <u>2</u>, <u>3</u>, 4, <u>5</u>, <u>6</u>, <u>9</u>, <u>10</u>

9) 1,325   2, 3, 4, <u>5</u>, 6, 9, 10

10) 78   <u>2</u>, <u>3</u>, 4, 5, <u>6</u>, 9, 10

11) 772   <u>2</u>, 3, <u>4</u>, 5, 6, 9, 10

12) 162   <u>2</u>, <u>3</u>, 4, 5, <u>6</u>, <u>9</u>, 10

13) 18   <u>2</u>, <u>3</u>, 4, 5, <u>6</u>, <u>9</u>, 10

14) 405   2, <u>3</u>, 4, <u>5</u>, 6, <u>9</u>, 10

15) 945   2, <u>3</u>, 4, <u>5</u>, 6, <u>9</u>, 10

16) 186   <u>2</u>, <u>3</u>, 4, 5, <u>6</u>, 9, 10

17) 640   <u>2</u>, 3, <u>4</u>, <u>5</u>, 6, 9, <u>10</u>

18) 150   <u>2</u>, <u>3</u>, 4, <u>5</u>, 6, 9, <u>10</u>

19) 350   <u>2</u>, 3, 4, <u>5</u>, 6, 9, <u>10</u>

20) 4,520   <u>2</u>, 3, <u>4</u>, <u>5</u>, 6, 9, <u>10</u>

21) 990   <u>2</u>, <u>3</u>, 4, <u>5</u>, <u>6</u>, <u>9</u>, <u>10</u>

22) 368   <u>2</u>, 3, <u>4</u>, 5, 6, 9, 10

23) 208   <u>2</u>, 3, <u>4</u>, 5, 6, 9, 10

24) 500   <u>2</u>, 3, <u>4</u>, <u>5</u>, 6, 9, <u>10</u>

Chapter 2:

Fractions

Adding Fractions – Unlike Denominator

Add the fractions and simplify the answers.

1) $\frac{1}{3} + \frac{1}{2} =$

2) $\frac{2}{7} + \frac{2}{3} =$

3) $\frac{3}{6} + \frac{1}{5} =$

4) $\frac{5}{13} + \frac{2}{4} =$

5) $\frac{3}{15} + \frac{2}{5} =$

6) $\frac{16}{56} + \frac{3}{16} =$

7) $\frac{3}{7} + \frac{2}{5} =$

8) $\frac{4}{12} + \frac{2}{5} =$

9) $\frac{6}{13} + \frac{3}{7} =$

10) $\frac{3}{8} + \frac{2}{5} =$

11) $\frac{1}{16} + \frac{4}{6} =$

12) $\frac{5}{24} + \frac{2}{3} =$

13) $\frac{3}{36} + \frac{5}{4} =$

14) $\frac{1}{25} + \frac{2}{5} =$

15) $\frac{7}{49} + \frac{3}{7} =$

16) $\frac{7}{12} + \frac{5}{6} =$

17) $\frac{3}{9} + \frac{2}{5} =$

18) $\frac{3}{45} + \frac{1}{5} =$

19) $\frac{3}{18} + \frac{7}{4} =$

20) $\frac{3}{10} + \frac{1}{4} =$

21) $\frac{3}{64} + \frac{1}{8} =$

22) $\frac{6}{14} + \frac{1}{3} =$

23) $\frac{2}{81} + \frac{1}{3} =$

24) $\frac{6}{15} + \frac{1}{3} =$

Subtracting Fractions – Unlike Denominator

Solve each problem.

1) $\dfrac{1}{2} - \dfrac{1}{3} =$

2) $\dfrac{5}{8} - \dfrac{2}{5} =$

3) $\dfrac{5}{6} - \dfrac{2}{7} =$

4) $\dfrac{3}{5} - \dfrac{1}{10} =$

5) $\dfrac{3}{5} - \dfrac{5}{12} =$

6) $\dfrac{5}{8} - \dfrac{5}{16} =$

7) $\dfrac{2}{25} - \dfrac{1}{15} =$

8) $\dfrac{3}{4} - \dfrac{13}{18} =$

9) $\dfrac{8}{5} - \dfrac{7}{6} =$

10) $\dfrac{5}{6} - \dfrac{2}{24} =$

11) $\dfrac{3}{4} - \dfrac{5}{36} =$

12) $\dfrac{1}{5} - \dfrac{2}{25} =$

13) $\dfrac{7}{6} - \dfrac{3}{18} =$

14) $\dfrac{7}{6} - \dfrac{5}{12} =$

15) $\dfrac{3}{5} - \dfrac{2}{9} =$

16) $\dfrac{3}{5} - \dfrac{1}{45} =$

17) $\dfrac{5}{32} - \dfrac{5}{48} =$

18) $\dfrac{2}{3} - \dfrac{2}{7} =$

19) $\dfrac{3}{5} - \dfrac{1}{6} =$

20) $\dfrac{3}{4} - \dfrac{5}{13} =$

Converting Mix Numbers

Convert the following mixed numbers into improper fractions.

1) $2\frac{3}{4} =$

2) $4\frac{12}{65} =$

3) $9\frac{3}{7} =$

4) $3\frac{5}{6} =$

5) $6\frac{6}{7} =$

6) $2\frac{10}{24} =$

7) $6\frac{7}{12} =$

8) $2\frac{12}{13} =$

9) $2\frac{12}{10} =$

10) $8\frac{6}{7} =$

11) $6\frac{1}{2} =$

12) $5\frac{14}{16} =$

13) $4\frac{8}{7} =$

14) $2\frac{9}{12} =$

15) $8\frac{3}{5} =$

16) $3\frac{4}{12} =$

17) $6\frac{3}{7} =$

18) $2\frac{1}{15} =$

19) $3\frac{7}{15} =$

20) $4\frac{3}{4} =$

21) $3\frac{5}{9} =$

22) $2\frac{11}{5} =$

23) $5\frac{13}{3} =$

24) $11\frac{7}{13} =$

Converting improper Fractions

Convert the following improper fractions into mixed numbers

1) $\frac{67}{12} =$

2) $\frac{75}{63} =$

3) $\frac{19}{15} =$

4) $\frac{58}{45} =$

5) $\frac{85}{26} =$

6) $\frac{271}{52} =$

7) $\frac{84}{63} =$

8) $\frac{41}{5} =$

9) $\frac{16}{15} =$

10) $\frac{11}{2} =$

11) $\frac{35}{4} =$

12) $\frac{120}{95} =$

13) $\frac{120}{54} =$

14) $\frac{28}{8} =$

15) $\frac{83}{11} =$

16) $\frac{31}{3} =$

17) $\frac{101}{8} =$

18) $\frac{51}{48} =$

19) $\frac{28}{9} =$

20) $\frac{8}{7} =$

21) $\frac{7}{2} =$

22) $\frac{43}{10} =$

23) $\frac{32}{24} =$

24) $\frac{78}{7} =$

Addition Mix Numbers

Add the following fractions.

1) $2\frac{1}{3} + 3\frac{1}{3} =$

2) $6\frac{3}{4} + 2\frac{1}{4} =$

3) $1\frac{1}{7} + 2\frac{2}{7} =$

4) $3\frac{1}{6} + 2\frac{3}{2} =$

5) $3\frac{4}{12} + 3\frac{3}{10} =$

6) $4\frac{1}{7} + 1\frac{1}{2} =$

7) $1\frac{2}{21} + 1\frac{2}{24} =$

8) $3\frac{2}{5} + 1\frac{3}{2} =$

9) $2\frac{3}{5} + 2\frac{1}{5} =$

10) $2\frac{4}{5} + 1\frac{3}{5} =$

11) $3\frac{2}{3} + 1\frac{3}{4} =$

12) $4\frac{1}{6} + 1\frac{3}{7} =$

13) $4\frac{1}{2} + 1\frac{3}{2} =$

14) $5\frac{3}{8} + 2\frac{1}{3} =$

15) $2\frac{3}{4} + 3\frac{1}{3} =$

16) $3\frac{1}{4} + 2\frac{3}{5} =$

17) $2\frac{3}{4} + 8\frac{2}{5} =$

18) $1\frac{3}{4} + 1\frac{1}{2} =$

19) $2\frac{3}{4} + 1\frac{1}{7} =$

20) $1\frac{2}{3} + 1\frac{3}{4} =$

21) $3\frac{1}{6} + 2\frac{1}{4} =$

22) $8\frac{2}{5} + 2\frac{3}{4} =$

23) $4\frac{2}{3} + 5\frac{1}{7} =$

24) $2\frac{1}{3} + 3\frac{2}{5} =$

Subtracting Mix Numbers

Subtract the following fractions.

1) $4\frac{1}{2} - 3\frac{1}{2} =$

2) $3\frac{3}{7} - 3\frac{1}{7} =$

3) $6\frac{3}{5} - 5\frac{1}{5} =$

4) $3\frac{1}{3} - 2\frac{1}{2} =$

5) $4\frac{1}{5} - 3\frac{1}{2} =$

6) $9\frac{1}{3} - 5\frac{2}{3} =$

7) $5\frac{5}{10} - 1\frac{6}{10} =$

8) $7\frac{4}{9} - 5\frac{8}{9} =$

9) $6\frac{2}{11} - 5\frac{5}{11} =$

10) $6\frac{2}{5} - 1\frac{1}{5} =$

11) $9\frac{1}{2} - 5\frac{1}{4} =$

12) $2\frac{5}{8} - 1\frac{3}{8} =$

13) $5\frac{3}{58} - 2\frac{5}{6} =$

14) $5\frac{1}{4} - 3\frac{1}{2} =$

15) $17\frac{1}{8} - 12\frac{3}{8} =$

16) $3\frac{3}{5} - 2\frac{1}{5} =$

17) $2\frac{1}{3} - 1\frac{2}{3} =$

18) $2\frac{1}{6} - 1\frac{2}{3} =$

19) $3\frac{2}{6} - 2\frac{1}{2} =$

20) $2\frac{5}{3} - 2\frac{1}{12} =$

21) $2\frac{9}{10} - 1\frac{1}{5} =$

22) $4\frac{2}{5} - 3\frac{1}{11} =$

23) $2\frac{1}{2} - 1\frac{1}{6} =$

24) $2\frac{3}{10} - 1\frac{4}{10} =$

Simplify Fractions

Reduce these fractions to lowest terms

1) $\dfrac{24}{16} =$

2) $\dfrac{18}{27} =$

3) $\dfrac{12}{15} =$

4) $\dfrac{36}{48} =$

5) $\dfrac{9}{27} =$

6) $\dfrac{15}{35} =$

7) $\dfrac{28}{49} =$

8) $\dfrac{80}{100} =$

9) $\dfrac{9}{81} =$

10) $\dfrac{25}{10} =$

11) $\dfrac{24}{32} =$

12) $\dfrac{20}{60} =$

13) $\dfrac{24}{40} =$

14) $\dfrac{3}{12} =$

15) $\dfrac{14}{49} =$

16) $\dfrac{52}{78} =$

17) $\dfrac{96}{36} =$

18) $\dfrac{48}{180} =$

19) $\dfrac{12}{32} =$

20) $\dfrac{88}{77} =$

21) $\dfrac{160}{320} =$

22) $\dfrac{24}{124} =$

23) $\dfrac{144}{36} =$

24) $\dfrac{120}{480} =$

Multiplying Fractions

Find the product.

1) $\frac{2}{7} \times \frac{3}{8} =$

2) $\frac{4}{25} \times \frac{5}{8} =$

3) $\frac{9}{40} \times \frac{10}{27} =$

4) $\frac{6}{13} \times \frac{22}{33} =$

5) $\frac{9}{12} \times \frac{3}{5} =$

6) $\frac{12}{17} \times \frac{5}{3} =$

7) $\frac{5}{6} \times \frac{6}{5} =$

8) $\frac{35}{89} \times 0 =$

9) $\frac{9}{4} \times \frac{12}{5} =$

10) $\frac{10}{18} \times \frac{3}{5} =$

11) $\frac{36}{25} \times \frac{25}{36} =$

12) $\frac{3}{36} \times \frac{6}{27} =$

13) $\frac{15}{7} \times \frac{3}{5} =$

14) $\frac{6}{7} \times \frac{3}{5} =$

15) $\frac{27}{14} \times \frac{7}{3} =$

16) $\frac{12}{17} \times 0 =$

17) $\frac{7}{11} \times \frac{33}{14} =$

18) $\frac{20}{9} \times \frac{3}{5} =$

19) $\frac{9}{16} \times \frac{4}{81} =$

20) $\frac{4}{23} \times \frac{2}{32} =$

21) $\frac{2}{12} \times \frac{3}{16} =$

22) $\frac{25}{8} \times \frac{2}{125} =$

23) $\frac{9}{16} \times \frac{4}{81} =$

24) $\frac{100}{200} \times \frac{400}{800} =$

Multiplying Mixed Number

Multiply. Reduce to lowest terms.

1) $1\frac{2}{3} \times 1\frac{1}{4} =$

2) $1\frac{2}{5} \times 1\frac{3}{2} =$

3) $1\frac{2}{3} \times 3\frac{1}{8} =$

4) $2\frac{1}{8} \times 1\frac{3}{5} =$

5) $2\frac{2}{3} \times 3\frac{1}{3} =$

6) $2\frac{1}{3} \times 1\frac{2}{3} =$

7) $1\frac{3}{4} \times 2\frac{1}{2} =$

8) $3\frac{2}{3} \times 2\frac{1}{3} =$

9) $2\frac{2}{3} \times 2\frac{1}{2} =$

10) $1\frac{1}{3} \times 1\frac{1}{2} =$

11) $2\frac{3}{4} \times 2\frac{2}{3} =$

12) $3\frac{2}{5} \times 2\frac{4}{7} =$

13) $1\frac{3}{4} \times 2\frac{1}{2} =$

14) $1\frac{1}{2} \times 3\frac{1}{7} =$

15) $1\frac{1}{2} \times 2\frac{1}{5} =$

16) $1\frac{2}{7} \times 2\frac{2}{3} =$

17) $1\frac{2}{3} \times 2\frac{1}{5} =$

18) $1\frac{2}{3} \times 3\frac{2}{5} =$

19) $1\frac{3}{4} \times 2\frac{1}{7} =$

20) $1\frac{1}{3} \times 3\frac{2}{5} =$

21) $1\frac{1}{2} \times 2\frac{1}{6} =$

22) $1\frac{1}{9} \times 1\frac{1}{7} =$

Dividing Fractions

Divide these fractions.

1) $0 \div \frac{1}{5} =$

2) $\frac{6}{12} \div 6 =$

3) $\frac{8}{11} \div \frac{3}{4} =$

4) $\frac{14}{64} \div \frac{2}{8} =$

5) $\frac{3}{19} \div \frac{9}{19} =$

6) $\frac{3}{12} \div \frac{15}{36} =$

7) $9 \div \frac{1}{5} =$

8) $\frac{15}{14} \div \frac{3}{7} =$

9) $\frac{6}{15} \div \frac{1}{14} =$

10) $\frac{2}{13} \div \frac{6}{5} =$

11) $\frac{5}{11} \div \frac{3}{10} =$

12) $\frac{15}{28} \div \frac{3}{7} =$

13) $\frac{7}{16} \div \frac{7}{4} =$

14) $\frac{6}{14} \div \frac{30}{7} =$

15) $\frac{8}{23} \div \frac{2}{23} =$

16) $\frac{9}{32} \div \frac{81}{4} =$

17) $\frac{5}{3} \div \frac{10}{27} =$

18) $8 \div \frac{1}{3} =$

19) $\frac{72}{32} \div \frac{3}{9} =$

20) $\frac{2}{30} \div \frac{8}{5} =$

21) $\frac{2}{9} \div \frac{6}{15} =$

22) $\frac{7}{21} \div \frac{3}{4} =$

Dividing Mixed Number

Divide the following mixed numbers. Cancel and simplify when possible.

1) $2\frac{1}{3} \div 2\frac{1}{2} =$

2) $3\frac{1}{8} \div 2\frac{2}{4} =$

3) $3\frac{1}{2} \div 2\frac{3}{5} =$

4) $2\frac{1}{7} \div 2\frac{1}{2} =$

5) $4\frac{1}{5} \div 2\frac{1}{3} =$

6) $2\frac{5}{9} \div 1\frac{2}{5} =$

7) $2\frac{2}{9} \div 1\frac{1}{2} =$

8) $3\frac{1}{7} \div 2\frac{1}{7} =$

9) $2\frac{1}{9} \div 2\frac{1}{2} =$

10) $3\frac{1}{6} \div 2\frac{2}{3} =$

11) $1\frac{2}{3} \div 5\frac{1}{3} =$

12) $3\frac{1}{9} \div 2\frac{2}{3} =$

13) $3\frac{1}{7} \div 1\frac{1}{11} =$

14) $9\frac{4}{7} \div 4\frac{1}{2} =$

15) $3\frac{3}{4} \div 2\frac{1}{2} =$

16) $2\frac{1}{3} \div 3\frac{2}{5} =$

17) $8\frac{3}{4} \div 2\frac{5}{8} =$

18) $3\frac{1}{3} \div 2\frac{3}{5} =$

19) $3\frac{2}{5} \div 2\frac{1}{2} =$

20) $5\frac{3}{8} \div 2\frac{1}{6} =$

21) $6\frac{1}{2} \div 2\frac{1}{4} =$

22) $4\frac{1}{5} \div 2\frac{1}{7} =$

23) $3\frac{1}{5} \div 2\frac{1}{5} =$

24) $2\frac{1}{7} \div 2\frac{1}{5} =$

Comparing Fractions

Compare the fractions, and write >, < or =

1) $\frac{15}{4}$ _____ $\frac{31}{12}$

2) $\frac{34}{5}$ _____ $\frac{1}{4}$

3) $\frac{3}{6}$ _____ $\frac{7}{5}$

4) $\frac{28}{7}$ _____ $\frac{14}{5}$

5) $\frac{1}{6}$ _____ $\frac{3}{5}$

6) $\frac{11}{7}$ _____ $\frac{15}{9}$

7) $\frac{6}{10}$ _____ $\frac{4}{7}$

8) $\frac{21}{12}$ _____ $\frac{23}{6}$

9) $2\frac{1}{10}$ _____ $5\frac{1}{2}$

10) $4\frac{1}{7}$ _____ $2\frac{1}{6}$

11) $2\frac{1}{3}$ _____ $2\frac{1}{4}$

12) $8\frac{6}{7}$ _____ $8\frac{2}{3}$

13) $1\frac{3}{7}$ _____ $2\frac{5}{3}$

14) $\frac{1}{13}$ _____ $\frac{4}{7}$

15) $\frac{41}{65}$ _____ $\frac{17}{43}$

16) $\frac{65}{200}$ _____ $\frac{65}{92}$

17) $12\frac{1}{2}$ _____ $12\frac{1}{7}$

18) $\frac{1}{2}$ _____ $\frac{1}{4}$

19) $\frac{1}{9}$ _____ $\frac{1}{15}$

20) $\frac{8}{14}$ _____ $\frac{6}{10}$

21) $\frac{5}{25}$ _____ $\frac{8}{56}$

22) $\frac{6}{7}$ _____ $\frac{3}{7}$

23) $1\frac{38}{32}$ _____ $2\frac{3}{16}$

24) $4\frac{18}{5}$ _____ $5\frac{4}{3}$

Answer key Chapter 2

Adding Fractions – Unlike Denominator

1) $\frac{5}{6}$

2) $\frac{20}{21}$

3) $\frac{7}{10}$

4) $\frac{23}{26}$

5) $\frac{3}{5}$

6) $\frac{53}{112}$

7) $\frac{29}{35}$

8) $\frac{11}{15}$

9) $\frac{81}{91}$

10) $\frac{31}{40}$

11) $\frac{35}{48}$

12) $\frac{7}{8}$

13) $\frac{4}{3}$

14) $\frac{11}{25}$

15) $\frac{4}{7}$

16) $\frac{17}{12}$

17) $\frac{11}{15}$

18) $\frac{4}{15}$

19) $\frac{23}{12}$

20) $\frac{11}{20}$

21) $\frac{11}{64}$

22) $\frac{16}{21}$

23) $\frac{29}{81}$

24) $\frac{11}{15}$

Subtracting Fractions – Unlike Denominator

1) $\frac{1}{6}$

2) $\frac{9}{40}$

3) $\frac{23}{42}$

4) $\frac{1}{2}$

5) $\frac{11}{60}$

6) $\frac{5}{16}$

7) $\frac{1}{75}$

8) $\frac{1}{36}$

9) $\frac{13}{30}$

10) $\frac{3}{4}$

11) $\frac{11}{18}$

12) $\frac{3}{25}$

13) 1

14) $\frac{3}{4}$

15) $\frac{17}{45}$

16) $\frac{26}{45}$

17) $\frac{5}{96}$

18) $\frac{8}{21}$

19) $\frac{13}{30}$

20) $\frac{19}{52}$

Converting Mix Numbers

1) $\frac{11}{4}$

2) $\frac{272}{65}$

3) $\frac{66}{7}$

4) $\frac{23}{6}$

5) $\frac{48}{7}$

6) $\frac{58}{24}$

7) $\frac{79}{12}$

8) $\frac{38}{13}$

9) $\frac{32}{10}$

10) $\frac{62}{7}$

11) $\frac{13}{2}$

12) $\frac{94}{16}$

13) $\frac{36}{7}$

14) $\frac{33}{12}$

15) $\frac{43}{5}$

16) $\frac{40}{12}$

17) $\frac{45}{7}$

18) $\frac{31}{15}$

19) $\frac{52}{15}$

20) $\frac{19}{4}$

21) $\frac{32}{9}$

22) $\frac{21}{5}$

23) $\frac{28}{3}$

24) $\frac{150}{13}$

Converting improper Fractions

1) $5\frac{7}{12}$

2) $1\frac{21}{63}$

3) $1\frac{4}{15}$

4) $1\frac{13}{45}$

5) $3\frac{7}{26}$

6) $5\frac{11}{52}$

7) $1\frac{21}{63}$

8) $8\frac{1}{5}$

9) $1\frac{1}{15}$

10) $5\frac{1}{2}$

11) $8\frac{3}{4}$

12) $1\frac{25}{95}$

13) $2\frac{12}{54}$

14) $3\frac{4}{8}$

15) $7\frac{6}{11}$

16) $10\frac{1}{3}$

17) $12\frac{5}{8}$

18) $1\frac{1}{16}$

19) $3\frac{1}{9}$

20) $1\frac{1}{7}$

21) $3\frac{1}{2}$

22) $4\frac{3}{10}$

23) $1\frac{1}{3}$

24) $11\frac{1}{7}$

Adding Mix Numbers

1) $5\frac{2}{3}$

2) 9

3) $3\frac{3}{7}$

4) $6\frac{2}{3}$

5) $6\frac{19}{30}$

6) $5\frac{9}{14}$

7) $2\frac{5}{28}$

8) $5\frac{9}{10}$

9) $4\frac{4}{5}$

10) $4\frac{2}{5}$

11) $5\frac{5}{12}$

12) $5\frac{25}{42}$

13) 7

14) $7\frac{17}{24}$

15) $6\frac{1}{12}$

16) $5\frac{17}{20}$

17) $11\frac{3}{20}$

18) $3\frac{1}{4}$

19) $3\frac{25}{28}$

20) $3\frac{5}{12}$

21) $5\frac{5}{12}$

22) $11\frac{3}{20}$

23) $9\frac{17}{21}$

24) $5\frac{11}{15}$

Subtracting Mix Numbers

1) 1

2) $\frac{2}{7}$

3) $1\frac{2}{5}$

4) $\frac{5}{6}$

5) $\frac{7}{10}$

6) $3\frac{2}{3}$

7) $3\frac{9}{10}$

8) $1\frac{5}{9}$

9) $\frac{8}{11}$

10) $5\frac{1}{5}$

11) $4\frac{1}{4}$

12) $1\frac{1}{4}$

13) $2\frac{19}{87}$

14) $1\frac{3}{4}$

15) $4\frac{3}{4}$

16) $1\frac{2}{5}$

17) $\frac{2}{3}$

18) $\frac{1}{2}$

19) $\frac{5}{6}$

20) $1\frac{7}{12}$

21) $1\frac{7}{10}$

22) $1\frac{17}{55}$

23) $1\frac{1}{3}$

24) $\frac{9}{10}$

Simplify Fractions

1) $\frac{3}{2}$

2) $\frac{2}{3}$

3) $\frac{4}{5}$

4) $\frac{3}{4}$

5) $\frac{1}{3}$

6) $\frac{3}{7}$

7) $\frac{4}{7}$

8) $\frac{4}{5}$

9) $\frac{1}{9}$

10) $\frac{5}{2}$

11) $\frac{3}{4}$

12) $\frac{1}{3}$

13) $\frac{3}{5}$

14) $\frac{1}{4}$

15) $\frac{2}{7}$

16) $\frac{2}{3}$

17) $\frac{8}{3}$

18) $\frac{4}{15}$

19) $\frac{3}{8}$

20) $\frac{8}{7}$

21) $\frac{1}{2}$

22) $\frac{6}{31}$

23) 4

24) $\frac{1}{4}$

Multiplying Fractions

1) $\frac{3}{28}$

2) $\frac{1}{10}$

3) $\frac{1}{12}$

4) $\frac{4}{13}$

5) $\frac{9}{20}$

6) $\frac{20}{17}$

7) 1

8) 0

9) $\frac{27}{5}$

10) $\frac{1}{3}$

11) 1

12) $\frac{1}{54}$

13) $\frac{9}{7}$

14) $\frac{18}{35}$

15) $\frac{9}{2}$

16) 0

17) $\frac{3}{2}$

18) $\frac{4}{3}$

19) $\frac{1}{36}$

20) $\frac{1}{92}$

21) $\frac{1}{32}$

22) $\frac{1}{20}$

23) $\frac{1}{36}$

24) $\frac{1}{4}$

Multiplying Mixed Number

1) $2\frac{1}{12}$

2) $3\frac{1}{2}$

3) $5\frac{5}{24}$

4) $3\frac{2}{5}$

5) $8\frac{8}{9}$

6) $3\frac{8}{9}$

7) $4\frac{3}{8}$

8) $8\frac{5}{9}$

9) $6\frac{2}{3}$

10) 2

11) $7\frac{1}{3}$

12) $8\frac{26}{35}$

13) $4\frac{3}{8}$

14) $4\frac{5}{7}$

15) $3\frac{3}{10}$

16) $3\frac{3}{7}$

17) $3\frac{2}{3}$

18) $5\frac{2}{3}$

19) $3\frac{3}{4}$

20) $4\frac{8}{15}$

21) $3\frac{1}{4}$

22) $1\frac{17}{63}$

Dividing Fractions

1) 0

2) $\frac{1}{12}$

3) $\frac{32}{33}$

4) $\frac{7}{8}$

5) $\frac{1}{3}$

6) $\frac{3}{5}$

7) 45

8) $\frac{5}{2}$

9) $\frac{28}{5}$

10) $\frac{5}{39}$

11) $\frac{50}{33}$

12) $\frac{5}{4}$

13) $\frac{1}{4}$

14) $\frac{1}{10}$

15) 4

16) $\frac{1}{72}$

17) $\frac{9}{2}$

18) 24

19) $\frac{27}{4}$

20) $\frac{1}{24}$

21) $\frac{5}{9}$

22) $\frac{4}{9}$

Dividing Mixed Number

1) $\frac{14}{15}$

2) $1\frac{1}{4}$

3) $1\frac{9}{26}$

4) $\frac{6}{7}$

5) $1\frac{4}{5}$

6) $1\frac{52}{63}$

7) $1\frac{13}{27}$

8) $1\frac{7}{15}$

9) $\frac{38}{45}$

10) $1\frac{3}{16}$

11) $\frac{5}{16}$

12) $1\frac{1}{6}$

13) $2\frac{37}{42}$

14) $2\frac{8}{63}$

15) $1\frac{1}{2}$

16) $\frac{35}{51}$

17) $3\frac{1}{3}$

18) $1\frac{11}{39}$

19) $1\frac{9}{25}$

20) $2\frac{25}{52}$

21) $2\frac{8}{9}$

22) $1\frac{24}{25}$

23) $1\frac{5}{11}$

24) $\frac{75}{77}$

Comparing Fractions

1) >	7) >	13) <	19) >
2) >	8) <	14) <	20) <
3) <	9) <	15) >	21) >
4) >	10) >	16) <	22) >
5) <	11) >	17) >	23) =
6) <	12) >	18) >	24) >

Chapter 3:

Decimal

Round Decimals

Round each number to the correct place value

1) 0.6̲4 =

2) 2.0̲4 =

3) 6.6̲23 =

4) 0.3̲77 =

5) 7̲.707 =

6) 0.08̲9 =

7) 6.2̲4 =

8) 76.76̲0 =

9) 1.62̲9 =

10) 10.3̲858 =

11) 1.0̲9 =

12) 4.2̲32 =

13) 3.2̲43 =

14) 6.05̲20 =

15) 63̲.69 =

16) 37̲.32 =

17) 41̲9.078 =

18) 512.6̲55 =

19) 12.36̲2 =

20) 65̲.65 =

21) 3.20̲89 =

22) 37.0̲73 =

23) 126.5̲16 =

24) 0.01̲22 =

25) 0.078̲5 =

26) 5.01̲62 =

27) 23.61̲33 =

28) 8.08̲20 =

Decimals Addition

Add the following.

1)
$$\begin{array}{r} 25.52 \\ + \ 52.25 \\ \hline \end{array}$$

2)
$$\begin{array}{r} 0.93 \\ + \ 0.07 \\ \hline \end{array}$$

3)
$$\begin{array}{r} 18.96 \\ + \ 12.87 \\ \hline \end{array}$$

4)
$$\begin{array}{r} 56.106 \\ + \ 3.198 \\ \hline \end{array}$$

5)
$$\begin{array}{r} 6.960 \\ + \ 5.87 \\ \hline \end{array}$$

6)
$$\begin{array}{r} 4.148 \\ + \ 3.231 \\ \hline \end{array}$$

7)
$$\begin{array}{r} 72.72 \\ + \ 12.87 \\ \hline \end{array}$$

8)
$$\begin{array}{r} 56.24 \\ + \ 23.47 \\ \hline \end{array}$$

9)
$$\begin{array}{r} 43.06 \\ + \ 11.87 \\ \hline \end{array}$$

10)
$$\begin{array}{r} 7.961 \\ + \ 12.87 \\ \hline \end{array}$$

11)
$$\begin{array}{r} 18.148 \\ + \ 12.231 \\ \hline \end{array}$$

12)
$$\begin{array}{r} 65.98 \\ + \ 8.37 \\ \hline \end{array}$$

13)
$$\begin{array}{r} 28.05 \\ + \ 7.37 \\ \hline \end{array}$$

14)
$$\begin{array}{r} 125.32 \\ + \ 3.32 \\ \hline \end{array}$$

Decimals Subtraction

Subtract the following

1) 8.97
    − 2.82
    _____

2) 84.02
    − 67.57
    _____

3) 0.65
    − 0.2
    _____

4) 9.784
    − 7.2
    _____

5) 0.784
    − 0.05
    _____

6) 84.62
    − 23.81
    _____

7) 121.26
    − 78.97
    _____

8) 24.36
    − 8.38
    _____

9) 52.59
    − 37.6
    _____

10) 5.872
    − 0.297
    _____

11) 61.43
    − 18.8
    _____

12) 17.732
    − 4.314
    _____

13) 23.502
    − 2.817
    _____

14) 135.35
    − 23.56
    _____

Decimals Multiplication

Solve.

1) $\begin{array}{r} 2.1 \\ \times\, 2.6 \\ \hline \end{array}$

2) $\begin{array}{r} 8.7 \\ \times\, 5.9 \\ \hline \end{array}$

3) $\begin{array}{r} 7.06 \\ \times\, 2.05 \\ \hline \end{array}$

4) $\begin{array}{r} 67.08 \\ \times\, 10 \\ \hline \end{array}$

5) $\begin{array}{r} 13.08 \\ \times\, 1000 \\ \hline \end{array}$

6) $\begin{array}{r} 32.06 \\ \times\, 7.8 \\ \hline \end{array}$

7) $\begin{array}{r} 26.12 \\ \times\, 12.01 \\ \hline \end{array}$

8) $\begin{array}{r} 4.06 \\ \times\, 7.05 \\ \hline \end{array}$

9) $\begin{array}{r} 18.06 \\ \times\, 0.05 \\ \hline \end{array}$

10) $\begin{array}{r} 21.09 \\ \times\, 9.07 \\ \hline \end{array}$

11) $\begin{array}{r} 14.3 \\ \times\, 15.7 \\ \hline \end{array}$

12) $\begin{array}{r} 5.12 \\ \times\, 0.03 \\ \hline \end{array}$

13) $\begin{array}{r} 8.05 \\ \times\, 0.21 \\ \hline \end{array}$

14) $\begin{array}{r} 12.12 \\ \times\, 5.03 \\ \hline \end{array}$

Decimal Division

Dividing Decimals.

1) $7 \div 1{,}000 =$

2) $3 \div 10 =$

3) $2.6 \div 1{,}000 =$

4) $0.01 \div 100 =$

5) $7 \div 49 =$

6) $2 \div 82 =$

7) $3 \div 48 =$

8) $8 \div 120 =$

9) $8 \div 100 =$

10) $0.8 \div 0.72 =$

11) $0.7 \div 0.07 =$

12) $0.9 \div 0.36 =$

13) $0.5 \div 0.35 =$

14) $0.6 \div 0.06 =$

15) $2.07 \div 10 =$

16) $7.6 \div 100 =$

17) $7.38 \div 1{,}000 =$

18) $15.6 \div 4.5 =$

19) $45.2 \div 5 =$

20) $0.3 \div 0.03 =$

21) $8.05 \div 2.5 =$

22) $0.05 \div 0.20 =$

23) $0.7 \div 4.4 =$

24) $0.08 \div 50 =$

25) $4.16 \div 0.8 =$

26) $0.08 \div 384 =$

Comparing Decimals

Write the Correct Comparison Symbol (>, < or =)

1) 1.15 _____ 2.15

2) 0.4 _____ 0.385

3) 12.5 _____ 12.500

4) 4.05 _____ 4.50

5) 0.511 _____ 0.51

6) 0.623 _____ 0.723

7) 8.76 _____ 8.678

8) 3.0069 _____ 3.069

9) 23.042 _____ 23.034

10) 6.11 _____ 6.08

11) 2.22 _____ 2.222

12) 0.06 _____ 0.55

13) 1.204 _____ 1.25

14) 4.92 _____ 4.0952

15) 0.44 _____ 0.044

16) 17.04 _____ 17.040

17) 0.090 _____ 0.80

18) 20.217 _____ 22.1

19) 0.021 _____ 0.201

20) 21.5 _____ 11.8

21) 3.5 _____ 10.9

22) 0.071 _____ 0.0701

23) 4.021 _____ 0.4021

24) 2.5 _____ 0.255

25) 5.2 _____ 0.255

26) 2.05 _____ 2.0500

27) 6.05 _____ 0.655

28) 1.0501 _____ 1.0510

Convert Fraction to Decimal

Write each as a decimal.

1) $\frac{40}{100} =$

2) $\frac{38}{100} =$

3) $\frac{4}{25} =$

4) $\frac{6}{24} =$

5) $\frac{9}{81} =$

6) $\frac{49}{100} =$

7) $\frac{2}{25} =$

8) $\frac{17}{25} =$

9) $\frac{47}{200} =$

10) $\frac{13}{50} =$

11) $\frac{18}{36} =$

12) $\frac{3}{8} =$

13) $\frac{6}{20} =$

14) $\frac{9}{125} =$

15) $\frac{27}{50} =$

16) $\frac{20}{50} =$

17) $\frac{45}{10} =$

18) $\frac{6}{30} =$

19) $\frac{67}{1,000} =$

20) $\frac{1}{10} =$

21) $\frac{7}{20} =$

22) $\frac{4}{100} =$

Convert Decimal to Percent

Write each as a percent.

1) $0.165 =$

2) $0.15 =$

3) $1.4 =$

4) $0.015 =$

5) $0.005 =$

6) $0.625 =$

7) $0.185 =$

8) $0.34 =$

9) $0.03 =$

10) $0.1 =$

11) $0.175 =$

12) $4.95 =$

13) $2.105 =$

14) $0.2 =$

15) $1.05 =$

16) $0.0275 =$

17) $0.0015 =$

18) $0.720 =$

19) $2.25 =$

20) $0.333 =$

21) $6.175 =$

22) $0.326 =$

23) $1.8 =$

24) $0.5 =$

25) $1.5 =$

26) $12.5 =$

27) $3.05 =$

28) $0.01 =$

Convert Fraction to Percent

Write each as a percent.

1) $\frac{1}{5} =$

2) $\frac{5}{4} =$

3) $\frac{8}{16} =$

4) $\frac{19}{22} =$

5) $\frac{14}{20} =$

6) $\frac{13}{50} =$

7) $\frac{7}{9} =$

8) $\frac{13}{20} =$

9) $\frac{5}{100} =$

10) $\frac{8}{20} =$

11) $\frac{3}{25} =$

12) $\frac{14}{100} =$

13) $\frac{48}{50} =$

14) $\frac{32}{50} =$

15) $\frac{19}{28} =$

16) $\frac{3}{33} =$

17) $\frac{24}{44} =$

18) $\frac{23}{28} =$

19) $\frac{24}{84} =$

20) $\frac{5}{50} =$

21) $\frac{25}{625} =$

22) $\frac{480}{240} =$

Answer key Chapter 3

Round Decimals

1) 0.6	11) 1.1	21) 3.21
2) 2.0	12) 4.2	22) 37.1
3) 6.6	13) 3.2	23) 126.5
4) 0.4	14) 6.05	24) 0.01
5) 8.0	15) 64.0	25) 0.079
6) 0.09	16) 37.0	26) 5.02
7) 6.2	17) 420.0	27) 23.61
8) 76.76	18) 512.7	28) 8.08
9) 1.63	19) 12.36	
10) 10.4	20) 66.0	

Decimals Addition

1) 77.77	6) 7.379	11) 30.379
2) 1	7) 85.59	12) 74.35
3) 31.83	8) 79.71	13) 35.42
4) 59.304	9) 54.93	14) 128.64
5) 12.83	10) 20.831	

Decimals Subtraction

1) 6.15	6) 60.81	11) 42.63
2) 16.45	7) 42.29	12) 13.418
3) 0.45	8) 15.98	13) 20.685
4) 2.584	9) 14.99	14) 111.79
5) 0.734	10) 5.575	

Decimals Multiplication

1) 5.46	6) 250.068	11) 224.51
2) 51.33	7) 313.7012	12) 0.1536
3) 14.473	8) 28.623	13) 1.6905
4) 670.8	9) 0.903	14) 60.9636
5) 1,3080	10) 191.2863	

Decimal Division

1) 0.007	2) 0.3	3) 0.0026

4) 0.0001

5) 0.142…

6) 0.024….

7) 0.0625

8) 0.0666…

9) 0.08

10) 1.111…

11) 10

12) 2.5

13) 1.4285…

14) 10

15) 0.207

16) 0.076

17) 0.00738

18) 3.4666…

19) 9.04

20) 10

21) 3.22

22) 0.25

23) 0.159…

24) 0.0016

25) 5.2

26) 0.0002

Comparing Decimals

1) <

2) >

3) =

4) <

5) >

6) <

7) >

8) <

9) >

10) >

11) <

12) <

13) <

14) >

15) >

16) =

17) <

18) <

19) <

20) >

21) <

22) >

23) >

24) >

25) >

26) =

27) >

28) <

Convert Fraction to Decimal

1) 0.4

2) 0.38

3) 0.16

4) 0.25

5) 0.11

6) 0.49

7) 0.08

8) 0.68

9) 0.235

10) 0.26

11) 0.5

12) 0.375

13) 0.3

14) 0.072

15) 0.54

16) 0.4

17) 4.5

18) 0.2

19) 0.067

20) 0.1

21) 0.35

22) 0.04

Convert Decimal to Percent

1) 16.5%

2) 15%

3) 140%

4) 1.5%

5) 0.5%

6) 62.5%

7) 18.5%

8) 34%

9) 3%

10) 10%   17) 0.15%   24) 50%

11) 17.5%   18) 72%   25) 150%

12) 495%   19) 225%   26) 1,250%

13) 210.5%   20) 33.3%   27) 305%

14) 20%   21) 617.5%   28) 1%

15) 105%   22) 32.6%

16) 2.75%   23) 180%

Convert Fraction to Percent

1) 20%   9) 5%   17) 54.5%

2) 125%   10) 40%   18) 82.14%

3) 50%   11) 12%   19) 28.57%

4) 86.36%   12) 14%   20) 10%

5) 70%   13) 96%   21) 4%

6) 26%   14) 64%   22) 200%

7) 77.8%   15) 67.9%

8) 65%   16) 9.09%

Chapter 4: Equations and Inequality

Distributive and Simplifying Expressions

Simplify each expression.

1) $4x + 1 - 5 =$

2) $-(-3 - 2x) =$

3) $(-2x + 3)(-1) =$

4) $(-x)(x - 2) =$

5) $-3x + x^2 - 3x^2 =$

6) $6y + 6x + 3y - 4x =$

7) $-2x + 2y + 10x - 8y =$

8) $-x - 7 + 5x + \frac{18}{3} =$

9) $3 - 4(x - 1) =$

10) $-4 - 4x + 6x =$

11) $(x - 2y)3 + 3y =$

12) $1.5x^2 \times (-6x) =$

13) $-3 - x^2 - 8x^2 =$

14) $6 + 10x^2 + 2 =$

15) $5(-3x - 6) + 12 =$

16) $(-x)(-1 + 2x) - 2x(2 + 3x) =$

17) $-4(7 + 10) - 2x + 4x =$

18) $-3(6 - 10x - 5x) =$

19) $2(-5x - 10) =$

20) $8 + 6x - 8 =$

21) $x(-x - 6) =$

22) $2xy + 3x - y + 2x + 3y =$

23) $2(-2x - 6) + 8 =$

24) $(-2x - 6) + 8 =$

25) $4x + 2y - 4 + 2 =$

26) $(-1 + 4x) - 2x(2 + 3x) =$

27) $(-2)(-2x - 2y) =$

28) $3(-2x - 1) + 8 =$

Factoring Expressions

Factor the common factor out of each expression.

1) $8x - 2 =$

2) $9x - 18 =$

3) $\frac{40}{20}x - 6 =$

4) $8b - 48 =$

5) $6a^2 - 30a =$

6) $3xy - 12y =$

7) $4x^2y + 8x =$

8) $a^2 - 5a + 6ab =$

9) $a^2 - ab =$

10) $6x + 9 =$

11) $10x - 40xy =$

12) $15x - 3 =$

13) $\frac{1}{5}x - \frac{2}{5}y =$

14) $8xy - \frac{16}{3}x =$

15) $2ab + 4c =$

16) $\frac{1}{2}x - \frac{3}{2} =$

17) $8x - 2xy =$

18) $x^2 + 5x =$

19) $3x^2 - 15y =$

20) $3x^3 + 2xy + x^2 =$

21) $16x - 8 =$

22) $40b - 80c - 40d =$

23) $27ab - 18ac =$

24) $ax - ay + 2x - 2y =$

25) $2ax + 3a + 4x + 6 =$

26) $x^2 - 9x =$

27) $7x^3 - 7x^2 =$

28) $4x^2 - 64xy =$

Evaluate One Variable Expressions

Evaluate each using the values given.

1) $x - 6x, x = 5$

2) $3(-4 + 2x), x = 2$

3) $2x + 10x, x = 2$

4) $2(3 - 2x) - 3, x = 2$

5) $3x + 2x - 8, x = 1$

6) $2x + 5x, x = 2$

7) $2x - 3x - 2, x = 4$

8) $\frac{2(2x+5)}{6}, x = 5$

9) $x - 54, x = 75$

10) $\frac{x}{16}, x = -80$

11) $2(7 + x) - 4, x = -7$

12) $5(x - 4) + 8, x = 5$

13) $\frac{x+(-5)}{-1}, x = -2$

14) $2(4 - 2x), x = 1$

15) $7 - \frac{x}{4} + 2x, x = 12$

16) $6x + 3x, x = 2$

17) $-9x + 6(8 + 4x), x = -6$

18) $x + 3x, x = 0$

19) $\frac{(3x-1)}{8}, x = 11$

20) $2(-2 - 3x), x = 4$

21) $6x - (6 - x), x = 2$

22) $\left(-\frac{18}{x}\right) + 1 + x, x = 9$

23) $-\frac{x \times 4}{x}, x = 3$

24) $3(-4 - 2x), x = 1$

25) $0.5x^2 + 6x, x = 2$

26) $8(2x + 2) - 3(x - 3), x = 2$

27) $-9x - 1, x = -3$

28) $3x + 9x, x = 2$

Evaluate Two Variable Expressions

Evaluate the expressions.

1) $2x + 3y$, $x = 5, y = 3$

2) $(-3)(-2x - 6y)$, $x = 2, y = 3$

3) $5x + y$, $x = 8, y = 6$

4) $\frac{x-2}{y+2}$, $x = 5, y = 1$

5) $\frac{a}{8} - 8b$, $a = 24, b = 3$

6) $3x + 2(2y - 3)$, $x = 3, y = 2$

7) $4x + 3y - 2$, $x = 5, y = 3$

8) $-2x + 5 + 6y - 3$, $x = 1, y = 2$

9) $yx \div 2$, $x = 7, y = 2$

10) $a - b \div 4$, $a = 5, b = 8$

11) $8(x - y)$, $x = 5, y = 2$

12) $9x - 2y$, $x = 3, y = 5$

13) $\frac{6}{a} + 4b$, $a = 3, b = 2$

14) $1.5x^2 + 6xy$, $x = 4, y = 2$

15) $7 - \frac{xy}{4} + 2y$, $x = 4, y = 2$

16) $8(2x - y)$, $x = 6, y = -2$

17) $6x^2 - 2y^2$, $x = 2, y = 3$

18) $5x + \frac{y}{2}$, $x = 2, y = 14$

19) $5(2x - 3y)$, $x = 2, y = 1$

20) $2x(y - \frac{2}{3})$, $x = 3, y = 1$

21) $3(x^2 - 5y)$, $x = 2, y = 1$

22) $6xy$, $x = 3, y = 7$

23) $\frac{1}{2}y^3 (y - \frac{2}{3}x)$, $x = 2, y = -1$

24) $-4(x - 8y) - 6x$, $x = 2, y = 1$

25) $-x + \frac{1}{2}xy$, $x = 2, y = 5$

26) $x^2 + xy^2$, $x = 6, y = 4$

27) $x - y + 6$, $x = 8, y = 4$

28) $\frac{xy}{x+y}$, $x = 4, y = 2$

Graphing Linear Equation

Sketch the graph of each line.

1) $y = 3x - 2$

2) $y = -3x + 4$

3) $x + y = 0$

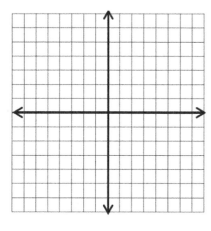

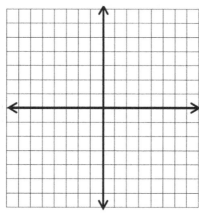

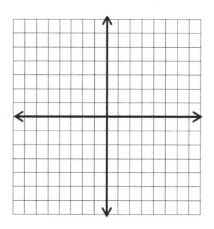

4) $x - y = -2$

5) $3x + 2y = -1$

6) $y - 2x + 4 = 0$

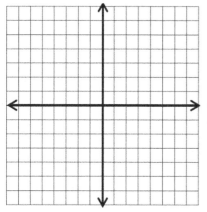

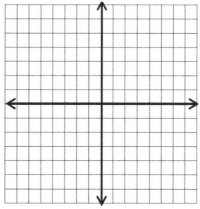

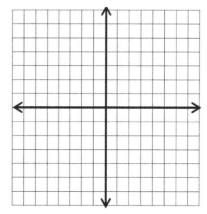

One Step Equations

Solve each equation.

1) $45 = (-10) + x$

2) $5x = (-40)$

3) $(-81) = (-9x)$

4) $(-6) = 2 + x$

5) $3 + \frac{x}{4} = (-2)$

6) $6x = (-96)$

7) $54 = x - 11$

8) $\frac{x}{4} = (-20)$

9) $x + 103 = 134$

10) $x - \frac{1}{2} = \frac{1}{2}$

11) $(-30) = x - 25$

12) $(-7x) = 49$

13) $(-144) = (12x)$

14) $-3x + 32 = 38$

15) $6x + 2 = 32$

16) $100 = (-10x)$

17) $2x + 6 = 2$

18) $25x = 500$

19) $x - 10 = 20$

20) $0.5x = 2.5$

21) $5x = 60$

22) $3x + 1.99 = 55.99$

23) $x + 6 = 4$

24) $x + 16 = 4$

25) $6x + 36 = 6$

26) $\frac{1}{5}x + 40 = 10$

Two Steps Equations

Solve each equation.

1) $5(2 + x) = 25$

2) $(-6)(x - 3) = 36$

3) $(-10)(2x - 2) = (-10)$

4) $6(1 + x) = -18$

5) $16(2x + 4) = 32$

6) $6(3x + 3) = 36$

7) $3(7 + 2x) = (-27)$

8) $(-10)(2x - 4) = 20$

9) $2(x + 10) = 30$

10) $\frac{2x - 3}{4} = 2$

11) $(-2) = \frac{x + 3}{6}$

12) $100 = (-5)(x - 2)$

13) $\frac{x}{2} + 5 = 11$

14) $\frac{1}{6} = \frac{1}{3} + \frac{x}{6}$

15) $\frac{12 + x}{4} = (-10)$

16) $(-2)(6 + 2x) = (-10)$

17) $(-5x) + 10 = 20$

18) $\frac{x + 6}{6} = -6$

19) $\frac{x + 20}{3} = 5$

20) $(-2) + \frac{x}{3} = (-12)$

21) $-3 = \frac{x + 5}{9}$

22) $\frac{3x - 5}{8} = 5$

23) $\frac{3x - 16}{6} = 3$

24) $20 = (-2)(x - 10)$

Multi Steps Equations

Solve each equation.

1) $1 - (3 - 2x) = 4$

2) $-10 = -(2x + 12)$

3) $7x - 13 = (-x) + 3$

4) $-42 = (-2x) - 12x$

5) $2(1 + 2x) + 2x = -16$

6) $4x - 10 = 3 + x - 5 + x$

7) $10 - 2x = (-32) - 2x + 2x$

8) $7 - 2x - 2x = 2 - 2x$

9) $5 + 9x + x = (-30) + 5x$

10) $(-2x) - 2(-1 + 5x) = 290$

11) $10 = (-100x) - 3 + 3$

12) $50 = 3x - 14 + 5x$

13) $5(1 + 5x) = 130$

14) $-30 = (-4x) - 6x$

15) $4(2x + 3) = -3(x - 1) + 31$

16) $5x - 8 = 2x + 4$

17) $10 = -(x - 6)$

18) $(-2) - 6x = 2(1 + 3x)$

19) $x + 1 = -3(2 + 2x)$

20) $6 = 1 - 2x + 3$

21) $7 - 5x - 2x = 12 - 2x$

22) $-3 + 4x + 3x = 24 - 11x$

23) $14 - 5x - 4x = 4 - 4x$

24) $10x - 16 = 4x + 8$

Graphing Linear Inequalities

Sketch the graph of each linear inequality.

1) $y > 3x - 5$ 2) $y < 2x + 1$ 3) $y \leq -4x - 5$

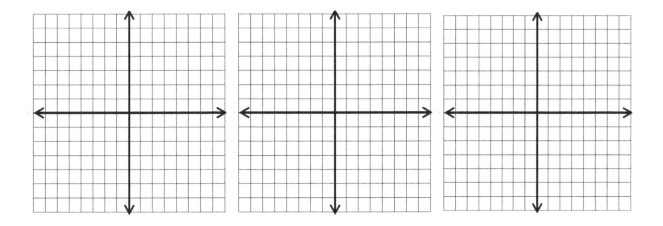

4) $4y \geq 12 + 4x$ 5) $-5y < x - 15$ 6) $3y \geq -9x + 6$

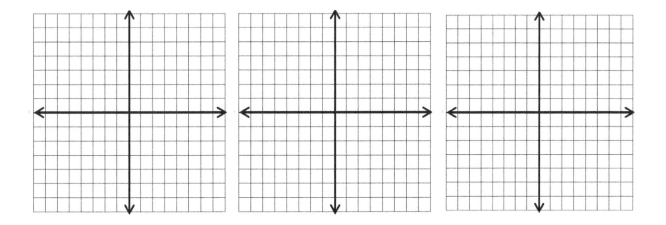

One Step Inequality

Solve each inequality.

1) $8x < 16$

2) $x + 5 \geq -10$

3) $x - 6 \leq 4$

4) $-x + 1 > -6$

5) $x + 12 \geq -12$

6) $x + 6 \geq 2$

7) $x - \frac{1}{2} \leq 4$

8) $-6x < 36$

9) $-x + 6 > -2$

10) $\frac{x}{2} + 2 > -8$

11) $-x + 6 > -3$

12) $x - 10 \leq 4$

13) $-x - 3 \leq -2$

14) $x + 24 \geq -10$

15) $x + \frac{1}{2} \geq -\frac{1}{2}$

16) $x + 5 \geq -15$

17) $x - 36 \leq -30$

18) $x - 3 \leq 4$

19) $-x + 5 > -8$

20) $x + 5 \geq -11$

21) $6x + 4 \leq 6$

22) $6x - 5 \geq 19$

23) $2x - 3 < 21$

24) $3x - 4 \leq 5$

Two Steps Inequality

Solve each inequality

1) $3x - 4 \leq 5$

2) $2x - 2 \leq 6$

3) $\frac{-2}{3}x + \frac{x5}{6} \leq \frac{1}{3}$

4) $2x + 7 \geq 21$

5) $3x - 5 \geq 10$

6) $2x - 4 \leq 2$

7) $8x - 4 \leq 4$

8) $7x + 3 \leq 10$

9) $3x + 9 > 12$

10) $\frac{x}{6} + 1 \leq 3$

11) $2x + 5 \geq 19$

12) $2x - 3 < 21$

13) $5 \geq \frac{x+2}{3}$

14) $2x + 4 < 24$

15) $\frac{4+x}{6} \geq 2$

16) $12 + 2x < 18$

17) $13 > 5\,x - 7$

18) $4 + \frac{x}{2} < 8$

19) $-3 + 3x > 21$

20) $6 + \frac{x}{5} < 2$

Multi Steps Inequality

Solve the inequalities.

1) $2x - 3 < 3x - 5$

11) $3x - 5 \leq 4x + 6$

2) $\frac{3x + 2}{2} \leq x$

12) $\frac{3x - 8}{7} > 1$

3) $6x - 7 > 2x + 17$

13) $7(x + 3) < 5x + 13$

4) $-2x > -5x + 2$

14) $-6x - 4 \leq 2(x - 10)$

5) $2 + \frac{x}{3} < \frac{x}{6}$

15) $\frac{3x - 2}{2} > 2x + 1$

6) $\frac{3x - 4}{7} > x$

16) $3(x - 6) + 2 \geq 5x - 4$

7) $3x - 18 + 2 > 5x - 4$

17) $\frac{-2x + 11}{10} > 2x$

8) $2x - 3 > 9 + 2(3x + 4)$

18) $-2x - 3 > -5x$

9) $\frac{x}{2} + 4 > x$

19) $\frac{2}{5}x - 15 > \frac{5}{8}x - 16$

10) $-5x + 6 \geq -7(5x - 6) - 6x$

20) $-2(x - 5) \leq 3x,$

Finding Distance of Two Points

Find the distance between each pair of points.

1) $(6, 3), (-3, -9)$

2) $(-8, -4), (8, 8)$

3) $(-6, 0), (30, 48)$

4) $(-8, -2), (2, 22)$

5) $(15, -10), (-30, -70)$

6) $(-24, 0), (-8, 12)$

7) $(9, 6), (33, 51)$

8) $(-18, -30), (18, -3)$

9) $(10, 18), (-22, -6)$

10) $(3, -1), (1, -3)$

11) $(1, 0), (6, 12)$

12) $(16, 8), (6, -16)$

13) $(12, 6), (-15, -30)$

14) $(-10, 12), (6, 42)$

15) $(0, 24), (-12, 15)$

16) $(-16, -10), (8, 0)$

17) $(9, 15), (-15, -30)$

18) $(-20, 16), (28, 36)$

Find the midpoint of the line segment with the given endpoints.

1) $(-1, -1), (0, 1)$

2) $(5, 2), (-1, 2)$

3) $(6, -1), (0, 5)$

4) $(-8, -2), (3, 3)$

5) $(2, -5), (6, -5)$

6) $(-6, -3), (2, -5)$

7) $(3, 0), (-3, 10)$

8) $(-3, 4), (-3, 0)$

9) $(-4, 4), (10, -6)$

10) $(0, 8), (8, -2)$

11) $(-6, 7), (4, 5)$

12) $(9, 6), (-1, -4)$

13) $(-4, 17), (-2, 1)$

14) $(12, 5), (8, -1)$

15) $(9, 8), (-3, 2)$

16) $(-7, -3), (-3, 9)$

17) $(15, 5), (3, 13)$

18) $(-4, -9), (10, -3)$

Answer key Chapter 4

Distributive and Simplifying Expressions

1) $4x - 4$

2) $3 + 2x$

3) $2x - 3$

4) $-x^2 + 2x$

5) $-2x^2 - 3x$

6) $2x + 9y$

7) $8x - 6y$

8) $4x - 1$

9) $-4x + 7$

10) $2x - 4$

11) $3x - 3y$

12) $-9x^3$

13) $-9x^2 - 3$

14) $10x^2 + 8$

15) $-15x - 18$

16) $-8x^2 - 3x$

17) $2x - 68$

18) $45x - 18$

19) $-10x - 20$

20) $6x$

21) $-x^2 - 6x$

22) $5x + 2y + 2xy$

23) $-4x - 4$

24) $-2x + 2$

25) $4x + 2y - 2$

26) $-6x^2 - 1$

27) $4x + 4y$

28) $-6x + 5$

Factoring Expressions

1) $2(4x - 1)$

2) $9(x - 2)$

3) $2(x - 3)$

4) $8(b - 6)$

5) $6a(a - 5)$

6) $3y(x - 4)$

7) $4x(xy + 2)$

8) $a(a - 5 + 6b)$

9) $a(a - b)$

10) $3(2x + 3)$

11) $10x(1 - 4y)$

12) $3(5x - 1)$

13) $\frac{1}{5}(x - 2y)$

14) $8x\left(y - \frac{2}{3}\right)$

15) $2(ab + 2c)$

16) $\frac{1}{2}(x - 3)$

17) $2x(4 - y)$

18) $x(x + 5)$

19) $3(x^2 - 5y)$

20) $x(3x^2 + 2y + x)$

21) $8(2x - 1)$

22) $40(b - 2c - d)$

23) $9a(3b - 2c)$

24) $(x - y)(a + 2)$

25) $(2x + 3)(a + 2)$

26) $x(x - 9)$

27) $7x^2(x - 1)$

28) $4x(x - 16y)$

Evaluate One Variable Expressions

1) -25

2) 0

3) 24

4) -5

5) -3

6) 14

7) -6

8) 5

9) 21

10) -5

11) -4

12) 13

13) 7

14) 4

15) 28

16) 18

17) -42

18) 0

19) 4

20) -28

21) 8

22) 8

23) -4

24) -18

25) 14   26) 51   27) 26   28) 24

Evaluate Two Variable Expressions

1) 19
2) 66
3) 46
4) 1
5) −21
6) 11
7) 27
8) 12

9) 7
10) 3
11) 24
12) 17
13) 10
14) 72
15) 9
16) 112

17) 6
18) 17
19) 5
20) 2
21) −3
22) 126
23) $1\frac{1}{6}$

24) 12
25) 3
26) 132
27) 10
28) $\frac{4}{3}$

Graphing Lines Using Line Equation

1) $y = 3x - 2$

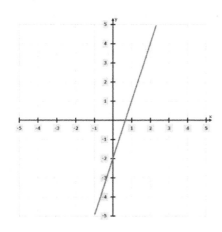

2) $y = -3x + 4$

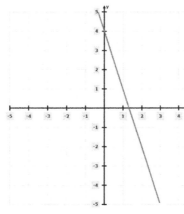

3) $x + y = 0$

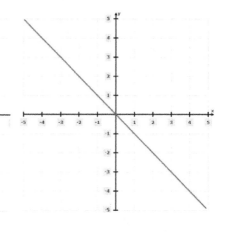

4) $x - y = -2$

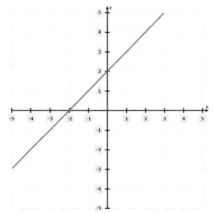

5) $3x + 2y = -1$

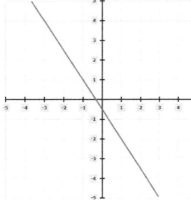

6) $y - 2x + 4 = 0$

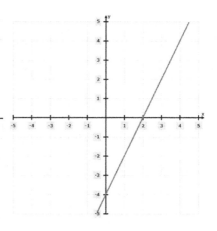

One Step Equations

1) $x = 55$	10) x = 1	19) x = 30
2) $x = -8$	11) x = −5	20) x = 5
3) $x = 9$	12) x = −7	21) x = 12
4) $x = -8$	13) x = 12	22) x = 18
5) $x = -20$	14) x = −2	23) $x = -2$
6) $x = -16$	15) x = 5	24) $x = -12$
7) x = 65	16) x = −10	25) $x = -5$
8) x = 80	17) $x = -2$	26) $x = -150$
9) x = 31	18) x = 20	

Two Steps Equations

1) $x = 3$	9) $x = 5$	17) $x = -2$
2) $x = -3$	10) $x = 5.5$	18) $x = -42$
3) $x = 1.5$	11) $x = -15$	19) $x = -5$
4) $x = -4$	12) $x = -18$	20) $x = -30$
5) $x = -1$	13) $x = 12$	21) $x = -32$
6) $x = 1$	14) $x = -1$	22) $x = 15$
7) $x = -8$	15) $x = -52$	23) $x = 11.33$
8) $x = 3$	16) $x = -0.5$	24) $x = 0$

Multi Steps Equations

1) $x = 3$	9) $x = -7$	17) $x = -4$
2) $x = -1$	10) $x = -24$	18) $x = -\frac{1}{3}$
3) $x = 2$	11) $x = -0.1$	19) $x = -1$
4) $x = 3$	12) $x = 8$	20) $x = -1$
5) $x = -3$	13) $x = 5$	21) $x = -1$
6) $x = 4$	14) $x = 3$	22) $x = 1.5$
7) $x = 21$	15) $x = 2$	23) $x = 2$
8) $x = 2.5$	16) $x = 4$	24) $x = 4$

Graphing Linear Inequalities

1) $y > 3x - 5$

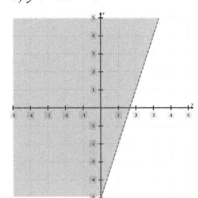

2) $y < 2x + 1$

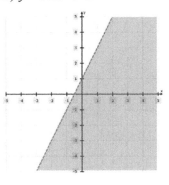

3) $y \leq -4x - 5$

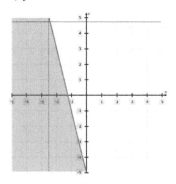

4) $4y \geq 12 + 4x$

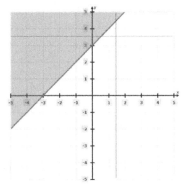

5) $-5y < x - 15$

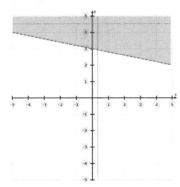

6) $3y \geq -9x + 6$

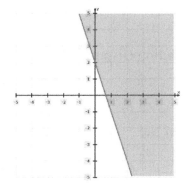

One Step Inequality

1) $x < 2$

2) $x \geq -15$

3) $x \leq 10$

4) $x < 7$

5) $x \geq -24$

6) $x \geq -4$

7) $x \leq \frac{9}{2}$

8) $x > -6$

9) $x < 8$

10) $x > -20$

11) $x < 9$

12) $x \leq 14$

13) $x \geq -1$

14) $x \geq -34$

15) $x \geq -1$

16) $x \geq -20$

17) $x \leq 6$

18) $x \leq 7$

19) $x < 13$

20) $x \geq -16$

21) $x \leq \frac{1}{3}$

22) $x \geq 4$

23) $x < 12$

24) $x \leq 3$

Two Steps Inequality

1) $x \leq 3$

2) $x \leq 4$

3) $x \leq 2$

4) $x \geq 7$

5) $x \geq 5$

6) $x \leq 3$

7) $x \leq 1$

8) $x \leq 1$

9) $x > 1$

10) $x \leq 12$

11) $x \geq 7$

12) $x < 12$

13) $x \leq 13$

14) $x < 10$

15) $x \geq 8$

16) $x < 3$

17) $x < 4$

18) $x < 8$

19) $x > 8$

20) $x < -20$

Multi Steps Inequality

1) $x > 2$

2) $x \leq -2$

3) $x > 6$

4) $x > \frac{2}{3}$

5) $x < -12$

6) $x < -1$

7) $x < -6$

8) $x < -5$

9) $x < 8$

10) $x \geq 1$

11) $x \geq -11$

12) $x > 5$

13) $x < -4$

14) $x \geq 2$

15) $x < -4$

16) $x \leq -6$

17) $x < \frac{1}{2}$

18) $x > 1$

19) $x < \frac{40}{9}$

20) $x \geq 2$

Finding Distance of Two Points

1) 15

2) 20

3) 60

4) 26

5) 75

6) 20

7) 51

8) 45

9) 40

10) $2\sqrt{2}$

11) 13

12) 26

13) 45

14) 34

15) 15

16) 26

17) 51

18) 52

Finding Midpoint

1) $(-0.5, 0)$

2) $(2, 2)$

3) $(3, 2)$

4) $(-2.5, 0.5)$

5) $(4, -5)$

6) $(-2, -4)$

7) $(0, 5)$

8) $(-3, 2)$

9) $(3, -1)$

10) $(4, 3)$

11) $(-1, 6)$

12) $(4, 1)$

13) $(-3, 9)$

14) $(10, 2)$

15) $(3, 5)$

16) $(-5, 3)$

17) $(9, 9)$

18) $(3, -6)$

Chapter 5:

Exponent and

Radicals

Positive Exponents

Simplify. Your answer should contain only positive exponents.

1) $2^3 =$

2) $5^3 =$

3) $\frac{2x^5y}{xy} =$

4) $(15x3x)^2 =$

5) $(x^3)^2 =$

6) $\left(\frac{1}{5}\right)^2 =$

7) $0^6 =$

8) $5 \times 5 \times 5 =$

9) $2 \times 2 \times 2 \times 2 \times 2 =$

10) $(3x^2y)^3 =$

11) $10^3 =$

12) $(2x^2y^4)^3 =$

13) $4 \times 10^3 =$

14) $0.5 \times 0.5 \times 0.5 =$

15) $\frac{1}{2} \times \frac{1}{2} \times \frac{1}{2} =$

16) $3^3 =$

17) $(10x^{10}y^3)^2 =$

18) $2^5 =$

19) $x \times x \times x =$

20) $3 \times 3 \times 3 \times 3 \times 3 =$

21) $(3x^2y^3z)^2 =$

22) $7^0 =$

23) $(12x^5y^{-2})^2 =$

24) $(3x^3y^2)^4 =$

Negative Exponents

Simplify. Leave no negative exponents.

1) $3^{-2} =$

2) $7^{-1} =$

3) $\left(\frac{1}{5}\right)^{-3} =$

4) $10^{-5} =$

5) $1^{-100} =$

6) $4^{-4} =$

7) $\left(\frac{1}{2}\right)^{-3} =$

8) $-5y^{-3} =$

9) $\left(\frac{1}{y^{-4}}\right)^{-2} =$

10) $x^{-\frac{3}{2}} =$

11) $\frac{1}{2^{-5}} =$

12) $3^{-4} =$

13) $2^{-3} =$

14) $15^{-1} =$

15) $20^{-2} =$

16) $x^{-4} =$

17) $(x^3)^{-2} =$

18) $x^{-1} \times x^{-1} \times x^{-1} =$

19) $\frac{1}{2} \times \frac{1}{2} =$

20) $10^{-2} =$

21) $10z^{-2} =$

22) $2^{-5} =$

23) $\left(-\frac{1}{3}\right)^4 =$

24) $6^0 =$

25) $\left(\frac{1}{x}\right)^{-4} =$

26) $12^{-2} =$

Add and subtract Exponents

Solve each problem.

1) $3^2 + 2^5 =$

2) $x^6 + x^6 =$

3) $3b^2 - 2b^2 =$

4) $3 + 4^3 =$

5) $8 - 4^2 =$

6) $4 + 7^1 =$

7) $2x^3 + 3x^3 =$

8) $10^2 + 3^5 =$

9) $4^5 - 2^4 =$

10) $5^2 - 6^0 =$

11) $1^2 - 3^0 =$

12) $7^1 + 2^3 =$

13) $6^1 - 5^3 =$

14) $3^3 + 3^3 =$

15) $9^2 - 8^2 =$

16) $0^{73} + 0^{54} =$

17) $2^2 - 3^2 =$

18) $7^3 - 7^1 =$

19) $8^2 - 6^2 =$

20) $4^2 + 3^2 =$

21) $2^3 + 4^3 =$

22) $10 + 3^3 =$

23) $6x^5 + 8x^5 =$

24) $8^0 + 4^2 =$

25) $3^2 + 3^2 =$

26) $10^2 + 5^2 =$

27) $(\frac{1}{2})^2 + (\frac{1}{2})^2 =$

28) $9^2 + 3^2 =$

Exponent multiplication

Simplify each of the following

1) $3^6 \times 3^2 =$

2) $9^2 \times 5^0 =$

3) $6^1 \times 7^3 =$

4) $a^{-3} \times a^{-3} =$

5) $y^{-2} \times y^{-2} \times y^{-2} =$

6) $2^4 \times 3^4 \times 2^{-2} \times 3^{-3} =$

7) $5x^2y^3 \times 8x^3y^5 =$

8) $(x^2)^3 =$

9) $(x^2y^3)^4 \times (x^2y^4)^{-4} =$

10) $6^3 \times 6^2 =$

11) $a^{2b} \times a^0 =$

12) $2^3 \times 2^4 =$

13) $a^m \times a^n =$

14) $a^n \times b^n =$

15) $6^{-2} \times 3^{-2} =$

16) $5^{12} \times 2^{12} =$

17) $(3^5)^4 =$

18) $\left(\frac{1}{5}\right)^3 \times \left(\frac{1}{5}\right)^2 \times \left(\frac{1}{5}\right)^4 =$

19) $\left(\frac{1}{7}\right)^{32} \times 7^{32} =$

20) $(2m)^{\frac{2}{3}} \times (-3m)^{\frac{2}{3}} =$

21) $(x^2y^3)^{\frac{1}{5}} \times (x^2y^2)^{\frac{1}{5}} =$

22) $(a^m b^n)^r =$

23) $(3x^2y^3)^4 =$

24) $(x^{\frac{1}{2}}y^3)^{\frac{-1}{2}} \times (x^2y^4)^0 =$

25) $6^3 \times 6^4 =$

26) $32^{\frac{1}{4}} \times 32^{\frac{1}{2}} =$

27) $8^4 \times 2^4 =$

28) $(x^3)^0 =$

Exponent division

Simplify. Your answer should contain only positive exponents.

1) $\dfrac{4^3}{4} =$

2) $\dfrac{25x^3}{x} =$

3) $\dfrac{a^m}{a^n} =$

4) $\dfrac{2x^{-5}}{10x^{-3}} =$

5) $\dfrac{81x^8}{9x^3} =$

6) $\dfrac{11x^6}{4x^7} =$

7) $\dfrac{18x^2}{6y^5} =$

8) $\dfrac{35xy^5}{x^5y^2} =$

9) $\dfrac{2x^5}{7x} =$

10) $\dfrac{36x^3y^7}{4x^4} =$

11) $\dfrac{9x^2}{15x^7y^9} =$

12) $\dfrac{yx^4}{5yx^7} =$

13) $\dfrac{14x^2y}{2xy^2} =$

14) $\dfrac{x^{3.25}}{x^{0.25}} =$

15) $\dfrac{5x^3y}{10xy^2} =$

16) $\dfrac{16ab^2r^9}{8a^3b^4} =$

17) $\dfrac{20x^3}{10x^5} =$

18) $\dfrac{16x^3}{4x^6} =$

19) $\dfrac{5^4}{5^2} =$

20) $\dfrac{x}{x^{12}} =$

21) $\dfrac{10^6}{10^2} =$

22) $\dfrac{2xy^4}{8y^2} =$

23) $\dfrac{12x^5y}{144xy^2} =$

24) $\dfrac{42x^6}{7y^8} =$

Scientific Notation

Write each number in scientific notation.

1) 8,100,000=

2) 50 =

3) 0.0000008 =

4) 254,000 =

5) 0.000225 =

6) 6.5 =

7) 0.00063 =

8) 19,000,000 =

9) 5,000,000 =

10) 85,000,000 =

11) 0.0000036 =

12) 0.00012 =

13) 0.005 =

14) 6,600 =

15) 1,960 =

16) 170,000 =

17) 0.115 =

18) 0.05 =

19) 0.0033 =

20) 20,000 =

21) 23,000 =

22) 0.00000102 =

23) 0.0102 =

24) 1,568 =

25) 32,581 =

26) 12,500 =

27) 12,054 =

28) 60,000 =

Square Roots

Find the square root of each number.

1) $\sqrt{1} =$

2) $\sqrt{4} =$

3) $\sqrt{16} =$

4) $\sqrt{25} =$

5) $\sqrt{49} =$

6) $\sqrt{81} =$

7) $\sqrt{100} =$

8) $\sqrt{144} =$

9) $\sqrt{121} =$

10) $\sqrt{169} =$

11) $\sqrt{9} =$

12) $\sqrt{36} =$

13) $\sqrt{225} =$

14) $\sqrt{196} =$

15) $\sqrt{256} =$

16) $\sqrt{625} =$

17) $\sqrt{289} =$

18) $\sqrt{1,024} =$

19) $\sqrt{484} =$

20) $\sqrt{361} =$

21) $\sqrt{441} =$

22) $\sqrt{841} =$

23) $\sqrt{729} =$

24) $\sqrt{900} =$

25) $\sqrt{400} =$

26) $\sqrt{3,600} =$

27) $\sqrt{4,900} =$

28) $\sqrt{6,400} =$

Simplify Square Roots

Simplify the following.

1) $\sqrt{72} =$

2) $\sqrt{27} =$

3) $\sqrt{28} =$

4) $\sqrt{44} =$

5) $\sqrt{50} =$

6) $\sqrt{40} =$

7) $10\sqrt{125} =$

8) $5\sqrt{600} =$

9) $\sqrt{18} =$

10) $3\sqrt{32} =$

11) $2\sqrt{5} + 8\sqrt{5} =$

12) $\frac{1}{1+\sqrt{2}} =$

13) $\sqrt{20} =$

14) $\frac{5}{2-\sqrt{3}} =$

15) $\sqrt{3} \times \sqrt{12} =$

16) $\frac{\sqrt{400}}{\sqrt{4}} =$

17) $\frac{\sqrt{48}}{\sqrt{16\times3}} =$

18) $\sqrt{24y^4} =$

19) $7\sqrt{64a} =$

20) $\sqrt{4+32} + \sqrt{16} =$

21) $\sqrt{90} =$

22) $\sqrt{338} =$

23) $\sqrt{60} =$

24) $\sqrt{75} =$

25) $\sqrt{1,875} =$

26) $\sqrt{32} =$

Answer key Chapter 5

Positive Exponents

1) 8

2) 125

3) $2x^4$

4) $2,025x^4$

5) x^6

6) $\frac{1}{25}$

7) 0

8) 5^3

9) 2^5

10) $27x^6y^3$

11) 1,000

12) $8x^6y^{12}$

13) 4,000

14) 0.5^3

15) $(\frac{1}{2})^3$

16) 27

17) $100x^{20}y^6$

18) 32

19) x^3

20) 3^5

21) $9x^4y^6z^2$

22) 1

23) $\frac{144x^{10}}{y^4}$

24) $81x^{12}y^8$

Negative Exponents

1) $\frac{1}{9}$

2) $\frac{1}{7}$

3) 125

4) $\frac{1}{100,000}$

5) 1

6) $\frac{1}{256}$

7) 8

8) $\frac{-5}{y^3}$

9) y^8

10) $\frac{1}{x^{\frac{3}{2}}}$

11) 2^5

12) $\frac{1}{81}$

13) $\frac{1}{8}$

14) $\frac{1}{15}$

15) $\frac{1}{400}$

16) $\frac{1}{x^4}$

17) $\frac{1}{x^6}$

18) $\frac{1}{x^3}$

19) $\frac{1}{2^2}$

20) $\frac{1}{100}$

21) $\frac{10}{z^2}$

22) $\frac{1}{32}$

23) $\frac{1}{81}$

24) 1

25) x^4

26) $\frac{1}{144}$

Add and subtract Exponents

1) 41

2) $2x^6$

3) b^2

4) 67

5) -8

6) 11

7) $5x^3$

8) 343

9) 1,008

10) 24

11) 0

12) 15

13) -119

14) 54

15) 17

16) 0

17) -5

18) 336

19) 28

20) 25

21) 72

22) 37

23) $14x^5$

24) 17

25) 18

26) 125

27) $\frac{1}{2}$

28) 90

Exponent multiplication

1) 3^8

2) 81

3) 2,058

4) a^{-6}

5) y^{-6}

6) $2^2 \times 3^1 = 12$

7) $40x^5y^8$

8) x^6

9) y^{-4}

10) 6^5

11) a^{2b}

12) 2^7

13) a^{m+n}

14) $(ab)^n$

15) 18^{-2}

16) 10^{12}

17) 3^{20}

18) $(\frac{1}{5})^9$

19) 1

20) $(-6m)^{\frac{2}{3}}$

21) $x^{\frac{4}{5}}y$

22) $a^{mr}b^{nr}$

23) $81x^8y^{12}$

24) $x^{\frac{-1}{4}}y^{\frac{-3}{2}}$

25) 6^7

26) $32^{\frac{3}{4}}$

27) $16^4 = 2^{16}$

28) 1

Exponent division

1) 4^2

2) $25x^2$

3) a^{m-n}

4) $\frac{1}{5x^2}$

5) $9x^5$

6) $\frac{11}{4x}$

7) $\frac{3x^2}{y^5}$

8) $\frac{35y^3}{x^4}$

9) $\frac{2x^4}{7}$

10) $\frac{9y^7}{x}$

11) $\frac{3}{5x^5y^9}$

12) $\frac{1}{5x^3}$

13) $\frac{7x}{y}$

14) x^3

15) $\frac{x^2}{2y}$

16) $\frac{2r^9}{a^2b^2}$

17) $\frac{2}{x^2}$

18) $\frac{4}{x^3}$

19) 5^2

20) $\frac{1}{x^{11}}$

21) 10^4

22) $\frac{1}{4}xy^2$

23) $\frac{x^4}{12y}$

24) $\frac{6x^6}{y^8}$

Scientific Notation

1) 81×10^5

2) 5×10^1

3) 8×10^{-7}

4) 2.54×10^5

5) 2.25×10^{-4}

6) 65×10^{-1}

7) 63×10^{-5}

8) 1.9×10^7

9) 5×10^6

10) 8.5×10^7

11) 3.6×10^{-6}

12) 1.2×10^{-4}

13) 5×10^{-3}

14) 6.6×10^3

15) 1.96×10^3

16) 1.7×10^5

17) 1.15×10^{-1}

18) 5×10^{-2}

19) 33×10^{-4}

20) 2×10^4

21) 23×10^3

22) 102×10^{-8}

23) 1.02×10^{-2}

24) 1.568×10^3

25) 32.581×10^3

26) 12.5×10^3

27) 1.2054×10^4

28) 6×10^4

Square Roots

1) 1

2) 2

3) 4

4) 5

5) 7

6) 9

7) 10

8) 12

9) 11

10) 13

11) 3

12) 6

13) 15

14) 14

15) 16

16) 25

17) 17

18) 32

19) 22

20) 19

21) 21

22) 29

23) 27

24) 30

25) 20

26) 60

27) 70

28) 80

Simplify Square Roots

1) $6\sqrt{2}$

2) $3\sqrt{3}$

3) $2\sqrt{7}$

4) $2\sqrt{11}$

5) $5\sqrt{2}$

6) $2\sqrt{10}$

7) $50\sqrt{5}$

8) $50\sqrt{6}$

9) $3\sqrt{2}$

10) $12\sqrt{2}$

11) $10\sqrt{5}$

12) $\sqrt{2} - 1$

13) $2\sqrt{5}$

14) $10 + 5\sqrt{3}$

15) 6

16) 10

17) 1

18) $2y^2\sqrt{6}$

19) $56\sqrt{a}$

20) 10

21) $3\sqrt{10}$

22) $13\sqrt{2}$

23) $2\sqrt{15}$

24) $5\sqrt{3}$

25) $25\sqrt{3}$

26) $4\sqrt{2}$

Chapter 6: Ratio, Proportion and Percent

Proportions

Find a missing number in a proportion.

1) $\dfrac{5}{8} = \dfrac{20}{a}$

11) $\dfrac{10}{8} = \dfrac{5}{a}$

2) $\dfrac{a}{6} = \dfrac{24}{36}$

12) $\dfrac{12}{a} = \dfrac{3}{17}$

3) $\dfrac{14}{42} = \dfrac{a}{3}$

13) $\dfrac{2}{7} = \dfrac{a}{10}$

4) $\dfrac{15}{a} = \dfrac{75}{32}$

14) $\dfrac{\sqrt{25}}{4} = \dfrac{30}{a}$

5) $\dfrac{8}{a} = \dfrac{32}{150}$

15) $\dfrac{12}{a} = \dfrac{13.2}{19.8}$

6) $\dfrac{\sqrt{16}}{5} = \dfrac{a}{30}$

16) $\dfrac{50}{190} = \dfrac{a}{380}$

7) $\dfrac{5}{12} = \dfrac{15}{a}$

17) $\dfrac{32}{100} = \dfrac{a}{52}$

8) $\dfrac{6}{12} = \dfrac{a}{33.6}$

18) $\dfrac{27}{81} = \dfrac{a}{3}$

9) $\dfrac{8}{a} = \dfrac{3.2}{4}$

19) $\dfrac{5}{8} = \dfrac{1}{a}$

10) $\dfrac{1}{16} = \dfrac{3}{a}$

20) $\dfrac{5}{3} = \dfrac{35}{a}$

Reduce Ratio

Reduce each ratio to the simplest form.

1) $3:12 =$

2) $4:24 =$

3) $81:45 =$

4) $30:25 =$

5) $24:240 =$

6) $80:10 =$

7) $80:400 =$

8) $5:180 =$

9) $24:72 =$

10) $3.6:4.2 =$

11) $220:660 =$

12) $1.8:3 =$

13) $150:250 =$

14) $40:60 =$

15) $26:52 =$

16) $16:4 =$

17) $100:25 =$

18) $10:100 =$

19) $108:72 =$

20) $130:165 =$

21) $30:60 =$

22) $24:28 =$

23) $10:150 =$

24) $15:90 =$

Percent

Find the Percent of Numbers.

1) 20% of 38 =

2) 42% of 7 =

3) 11% of 11 =

4) 36% of 75 =

5) 5% of 50 =

6) 32% of 14 =

7) 12% of 3 =

8) 9% of 47 =

9) 50% of 52 =

10) 7.5% of 60 =

11) 92% of 12 =

12) 80% of 60 =

13) 12% of 120 =

14) 1% of 310 =

15) 32% of 0 =

16) 62% of 100 =

17) 32% of 44 =

18) 15% of 60 =

19) 5% of 10 =

20) 3% of 7 =

21) 40% of 20 =

22) 70% of 2 =

23) 25% of 20 =

24) 7% of 200 =

25) 50% of 300 =

26) 3% of 6 =

27) 6% of 400 =

28) 9% of 6 =

Discount, Tax and Tip

Find the selling price of each item.

1) Original price of a computer: $250

Tax: 6%, Selling price: $_____

2) Original price of a laptop: $320

Tax: 5%, Selling price: $_____

3) Original price of a sofa: $400

Tax: 7%, Selling price: $_____

4) Original price of a car: $16,500

Tax: 4.5%, Selling price: $_____

5) Original price of a Table: $300

Tax: 6%, Selling price: $_____

6) Original price of a house: $450,000

Tax: 2.5%, Selling price: $_____

7) Original price of a tablet: $200

Discount: 20%, Selling price: $____

8) Original price of a chair: $250

Discount: 15%, Selling price: $____

9) Original price of a book: $50

Discount: 35% Selling price: $____

10) Original price of a cellphone: 600

Discount: 10% Selling price: $_____

11) Food bill: $32

Tip: 20%   Price: $_____

12) Food bill: $30

Tipp: 15%   Price: $_____

13) Food bill: $64

Tip: 20%   Price: $_____

14) Food bill: $36

Tipp: 25%   Price: $_____

Find the answer for each word problem.

15) Nicolas hired a moving company. The company charged $200 for its services, and Nicolas gives the movers a 30% tip. How much does Nicolas tip the movers? $_____

16) Mason has lunch at a restaurant and the cost of his meal is $60. Mason wants to leave a 10% tip. What is Mason's total bill including tip? $_____

Percent of Change

Find each percent of change.

1) From 200 to 400. ___ %

2) From 25 ft to 125 ft. ___ %

3) From $50 to $350. ___ %

4) From 40 cm to 160 cm. ___ %

5) From 20 to 60. ___ %

6) From 40 to 8. ___ %

7) From 160 to 240. ___ %

8) From 600 to 300. ___ %

9) From 75 to 45. ___ %

10) From 128 to 32. ___ %

Calculate each percent of change word problem.

11) Bob got a raise, and his hourly wage increased from $24 to $30. What is the percent increase? ____ %

12) The price of a pair of shoes increases from $60 to $96. What is the percent increase? ___ %

13) At a coffeeshop, the price of a cup of coffee increased from $2.40 to $2.88. What is the percent increase in the cost of the coffee? _____ %

14) 24cm are cut from a 96 cm board. What is the percent decrease in length? _ %

15) In a class, the number of students has been increased from 108 to 162. What is the percent increase? _____ %

16) The price of gasoline rose from $16.80 to $19.32 in one month. By what percent did the gas price rise? _____ %

17) A shirt was originally priced at $24. It went on sale for $19.20. What was the percent that the shirt was discounted? _____ %

Simple Interest

Determine the simple interest for these loans.

1) $225 at 14% for 2 years. $ _____

2) $2,600 at 8% for 3 years. $ _____

3) $1,300 at 15% for 5 years. $ _____

4) $8,400 at 2.5% for 5 months. $ ___

5) $300 at 2% for 9 months. $ _____

6) $48,000 at 5.5% for 5 years. $ ____

7) $5,200 at 9% for 2 years. $ _____

8) $600 at 5.5% for 4 years. $ _____

9) $800 at 4.5 % for 9 months. $ ____

10) $6,000 at 2.2% for 5 years. $ ___

Calculate each simple interest word problem.

11) A new car, valued at $14,000, depreciates at 4.5% per year. What is the value of the car one year after purchase? $_____

12) Sara puts $8,000 into an investment yielding 5% annual simple interest; she left the money in for two years. How much interest does Sara get at the end of those two years? $_____

13) A bank is offering 10.5% simple interest on a savings account. If you deposit $22,500, how much interest will you earn in two years? $_____

14) $800 interest is earned on a principal of $8,000 at a simple interest rate of 5% interest per year. For how many years was the principal invested? _____

15) In how many years will $1,500 yield an interest of $300 at 5% simple interest?

    _____

16) Jim invested $6,000 in a bond at a yearly rate of 3.5%. He earned $630 in interest. How long was the money invested? _____

Answer key Chapter 6

Proportions

1) $a = 32$

2) $a = 4$

3) $a = 1$

4) $a = 6.4$

5) $a = 37.5$

6) $a = 24$

7) $a = 36$

8) $a = 16.8$

9) $a = 10$

10) $a = 48$

11) $a = 4$

12) $a = 68$

13) $a = \frac{20}{7}$

14) $a = 24$

15) $a = 18$

16) $a = 100$

17) $a = 16.64$

18) $a = 1$

19) $a = 1.6$

20) $a = 21$

Reduce Ratio

1) $1:4$

2) $1:6$

3) $9:5$

4) $6:5$

5) $1:10$

6) $8:1$

7) $1:5$

8) $1:36$

9) $1:3$

10) $0.6:0.7$

11) $11:33$

12) $0.6:1$

13) $3:5$

14) $2:3$

15) $1:2$

16) $4:1$

17) $4:1$

18) $1:10$

19) $3:2$

20) $26:33$

21) $1:2$

22) $6:7$

23) $1:15$

24) $1:6$

Percent

1) 7.6

2) 2.94

3) 1.21

4) 27

5) 2.5

6) 4.48

7) 0.36

8) 4.23

9) 26

10) 4.5

11) 11.04

12) 48

13) 14.4

14) 3.1

15) 0

16) 62

17) 14.08

18) 9

19) 0.5

20) 0.21

21) 8

22) 1.4

23) 5

24) 14

25) 150

26) 0.18

27) 24

28) 0.54

Discount, Tax and Tip

1) $265.00	7) $240.00	13) $76.80
2) $336.00	8) $287.50	14) $45.00
3) $428.00	9) $67.50	15) $60.00
4) $17,242.50	10) $660.00	16) $66.00
5) $318.00	11) $38.40	
6) $461,250	12) $34.50	

Percent of Change

1) 100%	7) 50%	13) 20%
2) 400%	8) 50%	14) 25%
3) 600%	9) 40%	15) 50%
4) 300%	10) 75%	16) 15%
5) 200%	11) 25%	17) 20%
6) 80%	12) 60%	

Simple Interest

1) $63.00	7) $936.00	13) $4725.00
2) $624.00	8) $132.00	14) 2 *years*
3) $975.00	9) $27.00	15) 4 *years*
4) $87.50	10) $660.00	16) 3 *years*
5) $4.50	11) $13,370.00	
6) $13,200.00	12) $800.00	

Chapter 7:

Monomials and

Polynomials

Adding and Subtracting Monomial

Simplify each expression.

1) $x^2 + x^2 =$

2) $2x^2 + 3x^2 =$

3) $\frac{1}{5}x^3 + x^3 =$

4) $2\frac{1}{2}x^2 + 3\frac{1}{2}x^2 =$

5) $8x^2 - 3x^2 =$

6) $3.5x^5 - 1.5x^5 =$

7) $x^7 - x^7 =$

8) $(x^2)^3 + (x^2)^3 =$

9) $2x^{-3} + 5x^{-3} =$

10) $12p^5 + (-4p^5) =$

11) $x^{12} - 1.5x^{12} =$

12) $5\frac{1}{4}x^3 + 7\frac{1}{4}x^3 =$

13) $-2\frac{1}{5}x^{10} + 3\frac{1}{5}x^{10} =$

14) $\sqrt{64}p^5 + (-4p^5) =$

15) $(-3.6p^3) + (-2.4p^3) =$

16) $-x^3 + 6.5x^3 =$

17) $x^{12} + \frac{1}{2}x^{12} =$

18) $7x^3 - 2x^3 =$

19) $x^{12} - 4.5x^{12} =$

20) $8x^3 - 6x^3 =$

21) $12x^3 - 6x^3 =$

22) $16x^4 - 4x^4 =$

23) $2x^{-5} - 6x^{-5} =$

24) $10x^{-2} - 3x^{-2} =$

Multiplying and Dividing Monomial

Simplify.

1) $4xy^2 \times 3x^2 =$

2) $6xy \times 3x^2y =$

3) $2xy^2 \times (-4x^3y^2) =$

4) $8x^8y^9 \times x^2y^5 =$

5) $14x^3 \times (-4x^3) =$

6) $-4x^3y^2z \times 2x^3y^2z^5 =$

7) $-4 \times (-12x^{15}y^{12}) =$

8) $2x^3y^2 \times (-10x^3y^2) =$

9) $5x^3 \times (-7x) =$

10) $-9x^3y^{10} \times 6x^3y =$

11) $24x^{-3}y^5 \times (-x^{-8}y^{-2}) =$

12) $10x^{12}y^2z \times 3xy^{-2}z =$

13) $\frac{40x^{12}y^9}{20x^6y^7} =$

14) $(9x^{-3}y^4)^{-2} =$

15) $\frac{140x^{16}y^8}{5x^9y^2} =$

16) $\frac{20x^{12}}{5x^7} =$

17) $\frac{24x^8y^5z^5}{8x^3y^5z} =$

18) $\frac{12x^2+6x}{3x} =$

19) $\frac{100x^3y^8}{50x^3y^7} =$

20) $(14x^3)(10x^9) =$

21) $\frac{24x^2y^5+6xy^8}{3xy} =$

22) $\frac{-64x^5y^{10}}{8x^3y^7} =$

23) $\frac{12x^4y^{10}}{8x^2y^3} =$

24) $\frac{32x^{15}y^{10}z}{8x^3y^3} =$

Binomial Operations

Solve each operation below.

1) $2x + 6 - (5x - 2) =$

2) $(3x - 8) + (2x - 6) =$

3) $(-3x - 3) + (5x + 4) =$

4) $(3x - 1.2) + (6x - 2.4) =$

5) $\frac{1}{5}x + 3 - \left(\frac{1}{2}x - 2\right) =$

6) $4x + 1 - (2x - 3) =$

7) $16x + 3 - (24x - 2) =$

8) $(x + 5)(x + 6) =$

9) $(x - 5)(x - 4) =$

10) $(x - 6)(2x + 2) =$

11) $(x - 6)(x + 6) =$

12) $(x - 4)(4x + 3) =$

13) $(2x - 3)(2x + 3) =$

14) $(x + 5)(x - 2) =$

15) $(x - 2)(3x + 2) =$

16) $(x^2 + 2)(x^2 - 2) =$

17) $(x - 5)(x + 5) =$

18) $5x(8x - 5) =$

19) $12x(2x + 8) =$

20) $(4x + 5) + (3x - 8) + (2x - 6) =$

21) $(x^2 + 1)(x^2 - 1)$

22) $(2x - 5)(4x + 2)$

23) $(x - 3)(8x + 1)$

24) $(x - 1.2)(2.4x + 1.2)$

Polynomial Operations

Simplify each expression.

1) $(5x^2 + 2x - 8) + (3x - 6x^2 - 5) =$

2) $(4x^2 + 3x - 4) - (2x - 4x^2 - 1) =$

3) $(10x^2 - 6x + 4) - (-3x + 8x^2 - 2) =$

4) $(4x^5 - 3x^3 - 6x) + (6x + 10x^4 - 12) + (2x^2 + x^3 + 14) =$

5) $(12x^2 - 9x + 6) + (8x^2 - 3x + 1) =$

6) $10(2x^2 - 5x - 4) =$

7) $2x^3(2x^2 - 2x + 1) =$

8) $2x^2y^2(4x^2 - 5x + 2) =$

9) $(x + 6)(x^2 - 8x + 9) =$

10) $x(2x^2 - 2x + 8) =$

11) $8(x^2 - 2x + 3) =$

12) $(x - 2)(x^2 + 3x - 1) =$

13) $(10x^3 + 4x^2 - 12) + (-4x^3 + 5x^2 + 10) =$

14) $(2x - 1)(2x^2 + 3x + 8) =$

Squaring a Binomial

Write each square as a trinomial.

1) $(a + b)^2 =$

2) $(x + 3)^2 =$

3) $(a - b)^2 =$

4) $(2x + 1)^2 =$

5) $(2x - 9)^2 =$

6) $(x + \frac{3}{2})^2 =$

7) $(2x - 3y)^2 =$

8) $(x - 3)^2 =$

9) $(x + 2)^2 =$

10) $(3x - 7)^2 =$

11) $(2x + 2y)^2 =$

12) $(x + 1)^2 =$

13) $(x + \frac{1}{2})^2 =$

14) $(x^2 + y^2)^2 =$

15) $(x - 10)^2 =$

16) $\left(x + \sqrt{2}\right)^2 =$

17) $(5x - 3)^2 =$

18) $(x + 4)^2 =$

19) $(9x - 2y)^2 =$

20) $(x + 9)^2 =$

21) $5(x + 1)^2 =$

22) $(x^2 - 4)^2 =$

23) $(x + 6)^2 =$

24) $(3x + 1)^2 =$

Factor polynomial

Factor each completely.

1) $x^2 + 8x + 15 =$

11) $2x^2 - 13x + 15 =$

2) $16x^2 - 32x =$

12) $\frac{2x^2 - x - 15}{x^2 - 2x - 3} =$

3) $x^3 - 4x^2 - 4x + 16 =$

13) $\frac{(x-2)(x-6)}{(x-2)(x-7)} =$

4) $x^2 + 9x + 18 =$

14) $(x - 3)3x + (x - 3)3 =$

5) $x^4 - 4x^2 - 21 =$

15) $12x^2 - 63x^4 =$

6) $x^2 - 10x - 16 =$

16) $\frac{x^2 + 7x + 12}{(x+3)} =$

7) $6 + 2x + 14 + 3x =$

17) $x^2 + 3x - 10 =$

8) $5x^2 - 15x + 2x - 6 =$

18) $3x^4 + 9x^2 - 6x^3 - 18x =$

9) $14x^3y + 7x^2y - 7xy =$

19) $10(a + b) - 3a(a + b) =$

10) $6x^2 - 8x - 8 =$

20) $10x^2 - 20x =$

Answer key Chapter 7

Adding and Subtracting Monomial

1) $2x^2$

2) $5x^2$

3) $\frac{6}{5}x^3$

4) $6x^2$

5) $5x^2$

6) $2x^5$

7) 0

8) $2x^6$

9) $7x^{-3}$

10) $8p^5$

11) $-0.5x^{12}$

12) $12\frac{1}{2}x^3$

13) x^{10}

14) $4p^5$

15) $-6p^3$

16) $-5.5x^{13}$

17) $\frac{3}{2}x^{12}$

18) $5x^3$

19) $-3.5x^{12}$

20) $2x^3$

21) $6x^3$

22) $12x^4$

23) $-4x^{-5}$

24) $7x^{-2}$

Multiplying and Dividing Monomial

1) $12x^3y^2$

2) $18x^3y^2$

3) $-8x^4y^4$

4) $8x^{10}y^{14}$

5) $-56x^6$

6) $-8x^6y^4z^6$

7) $48x^{15}y^{12}$

8) $-20x^6y^4$

9) $-35x^4$

10) $-54x^6y^{11}$

11) $-24x^{-11}y^3$

12) $30x^{13}z^2$

13) $2x^6y^2$

14) $\frac{1}{81}x^6y^{-8}$

15) $28x^7y^6$

16) $4x^5$

17) $3x^5z^4$

18) $4x + 2$

19) $2y$

20) $140x^{12}$

21) $8xy^4 + 2y^7$

22) $-8x^2y^3$

23) $\frac{3}{2}x^2y^7$

24) $4x^{12}y^7z$

Binomial Operations

1) $-3x + 8$

2) $5x - 14$

3) $2x + 1$

4) $9x - 3.6$

5) $-\frac{3}{10}x + 5$

6) $2x + 4$

7) $-8x + 5$

8) $x^2 + 11x + 30$

9) $x^2 - 9x + 20$

10) $2x^2 - 10x - 12$

11) $x^2 - 36$

12) $4x^2 - 13x - 12$

13) $4x^2 - 9$

14) $x^2 + 3x - 10$

15) $3x^2 - 4x - 4$

16) $x^4 - 4$

17) $x^2 - 25$

18) $40x^2 - 25x$

19) $24x^2 + 96x$

20) $9x - 9$

21) $x^4 - 1$

22) $8x^2 - 16x - 10$

23) $8x^2 - 23x - 3$

24) $2.4x^2 - 1.68x - 1.44$

Polynomial Operations

1) $-x^2 + 5x - 13$

2) $8x^2 + x - 3$

3) $2x^2 - 3x + 6$

4) $4x^5 + 10x^4 - 2x^3 + 2x^2 + 2$

5) $20x^2 - 12x + 7$

6) $20x^2 - 50x - 40$

7) $4x^5 - 4x^4 + 2x^3$

8) $8x^4y^2 - 10x^3y^2 + 4x^2y^2$

9) $x^3 - 2x^2 - 39x + 54$

10) $2x^3 - 2x^2 + 8x$

11) $8x^2 - 16x + 24$

12) $x^3 + x^2 - 7x + 2$

13) $6x^3 + 9x^2 - 2$

14) $4x^3 + 4x^2 + 13x - 8$

Squaring a Binomial

1) $a^2 + b^2 + 2ab$

2) $x^2 + 6x + 9$

3) $a^2 + b^2 - 2ab$

4) $4x^2 + 4x + 1$

5) $4x^2 - 36x + 81$

6) $x^2 + 3x + \frac{9}{4}$

7) $4x^2 - 12xy + 9y^2$

8) $x^2 - 6x + 9$

9) $x^2 + 4x + 4$

10) $9x^2 - 42x + 49$

11) $4x^2 + 8xy + 4y^2$

12) $x^2 + 2x + 1$

13) $x^2 + x + \frac{1}{4}$

14) $x^4 + y^4 + 2x^2y^2$

15) $x^2 - 20x + 100$

16) $x^2 + 2\sqrt{2}x + 2$

17) $25x^2 - 30x + 9$

18) $x^2 + 8x + 16$

19) $81x^2 - 36xy + 4y^2$

20) $x^2 + 18x + 81$

21) $5x^2 + 10x + 5$

22) $x^4 - 8x^2 + 16$

23) $x^2 + 12x + 36$

24) $9x^2 + 6x + 1$

Factor polynomial

1) $(x + 5)(x + 3)$

2) $16x(x - 2)$

3) $(x^2 - 4)(x - 4)$

4) $(x + 3)(x + 6)$

5) $(x^2 - 7)(x^2 + 3)$

6) $(x - 8)(x - 2)$

7) $5(x + 4)$

8) $5x(x - 3) + 2(x - 3)$

9) $7xy(2x^2 + x - 1)$

10) $(3x + 2)(2x - 4)$

11) $(2x - 3)(x - 5)$

12) $\frac{2x+5}{x+1}$

13) $\frac{x-6}{x-7}$

14) $(x - 3)(3x + 3)$

15) $-3x^2(-4 + 21x^2)$

16) $x + 4$

17) $(x + 5)(x - 2)$

18) $3x(x^2 + 3)(x - 2)$

19) $(a + b)(10 - 3a)$

20) $10x(x - 2)$

Chapter 8:

Functions

Relation and Functions

Determine whether each relation is a function. Then state the domain and range of each relation.

1)

Function:

....

Domain:

....

Range:

....

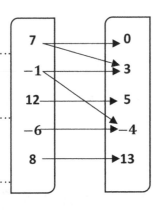

2)

Function:

....

Domain:

....

Range:

....

x	y
3	3
6	0
−1	−1
4	−1
−3	1

4) $\{(1, -1), (2, -3), (4, 4), (3, 0), (2, 5)\}$

3)

Function:

....

Domain:

....

Range:

....

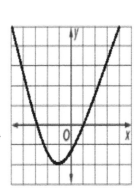

Function:

....

Domain:

....

Range:

....

5)

Function:

....

Domain:

....

Range:

....

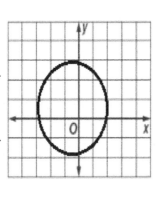

6)

Function:

....

Domain:

....

Range:

....

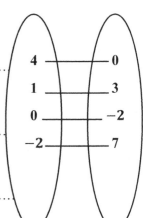

Slope form

Write the slope-intercept form of the equation of each line.

1) $2x + 3y = 12$

2) $x + 10y = 5$

3) $2x + y = -3$

4) $-6x + 5y = 12$

5) $3x - 2y = 21$

6) $-49x + 7y = 14$

7) $x + y = 0$

8) $10x - 11y = -8$

9) $-4.5x + 9y = 18$

10) $-6x + \frac{3}{4}y = 9$

11) $8x + \frac{4}{5}y = -12$

12) $x = -12y - 9$

13) $0.5x = y + 1$

14) $3x = -\frac{3}{4}y + 15$

Slope and Y-Intercept

Find the slope and y-intercept of each equation.

1) $y = \frac{1}{7}x + 1$

2) $y = 5x + 6$

3) $x - 2y = 6$

4) $y = 4x + 32$

5) $y = 5$

6) $y = -x + 1$

7) $x = -12$

8) $y = 3x$

9) $y - 2 = 3(x + 1)$

10) $x = -\frac{4}{7}y - \frac{1}{6}$

Slope and One Point

Find a Point-Slope equation for a line containing the given point and having the given slope.

1) $m = -1, (3, -2)$

2) $m = 4, (1,3)$

3) $m = -1, (-3, -7)$

4) $m = 2, (4,0)$

5) $m = 7, (1,2)$

6) $m = \frac{5}{2}, (2,9)$

7) $m = 0, (-1, -2)$

8) $m = 1, (0, -1)$

9) $m = 2, (1,5)$

10) $m = \frac{2}{5}, (-4, -2)$

11) $m = -4, (-1, -2)$

12) $m = -1, (3, -2)$

13) $m = 3, (1, -1)$

14) $m =$ undefined, $(3, -2)$

15) $m = -\frac{1}{6}, (6,3)$

16) $m = \frac{1}{6}, (5,1)$

17) $m = -9, (3,4)$

18) $m = 4, (-1, -5)$

19) $m = \frac{1}{2}, (0,1)$

20) $m = \frac{-3}{7}, (1, -2)$

21) $m = \frac{1}{2}, (0,0)$

22) $m = -2, (1, -1)$

23) $m = 0, (0.5, -2)$

24) $m = -\frac{3}{4}, (6, -4)$

25) $m = 0, (-1,0)$

26) $m =$ Undefined, $(-4, -1)$

Slope of Two Points

Write the slope-intercept form of the equation of the line through the given points.

1) $(0,0), (2,3)$

2) $(0,-2), (3,4)$

3) $(-3,0), (0,3)$

4) $(1,-6), (-5,3)$

5) $(3,0), (4,0)$

6) $(2,-7), (-5,0)$

7) $(3,4), (2,6)$

8) $(-2,3), (6,-1)$

9) $(6,3), (2,-1)$

10) $(8,0), (8,-1)$

11) $(-1,5), (2,3)$

12) $(4,-3), (3,-3)$

13) $(4,1), (-6,4)$

14) $(0,-2), (5,2)$

15) $(-7,+4), (-10,1)$

16) $(5,3), (7,2)$

17) $(-1,0), (1,-2)$

18) $(1,-7), (-5,0)$

19) $(-2,-2), (4,1)$

20) $(-2,-2), (3,8)$

21) $(5,-2), (2,10)$

22) $(3,8), (7,12)$

23) $(1,3), (4,0)$

24) $(1,2), (2,0)$

Equation of Parallel and Perpendicular lines

Write the slope-intercept form of the equation of the line described.

1) Through: $(2, 2)$, parallel to $y = x + 4$

2) Through: $(5, 3)$, parallel to $x = 0$

3) Through: $(1, -8)$, perpendecular to $y = \frac{1}{7}x + 6$

4) Through: $(3, 3)$, parallel to $y = -6x + 2$

5) Through: $(-1, 3)$, parallel to $y = \frac{5}{9}x + 4$

6) Through: $(3, 1)$, perpendecular to $y = -\frac{1}{9}x + 3$

7) Through: $(6, 4)$, perpendecular to $y = -2x + 8$

8) Through: $(-2, 6)$, perpendecular to $y = -\frac{1}{4}x + 3$

9) Through: $(2, 3)$, parallel to $y + x = 1$

10) Through: $(4, -2)$, parallel to $y = \frac{1}{4}x$

11) Through: $(3, -3)$, parallel to $y = 4$

12) Through: $(0, 3)$, perpendecular to $y = \frac{3}{2}x + 1$

13) Through: $(4, 3)$, perpendecular to $y + x = -5$

14) Through: $(4, 2)$, parallel to $4y - x = 3\frac{1}{2}$

15) Through: $(0, 0)$, perpendecular to $y = 2x + 6$

16) Through: $(-2, 7)$, parallel to $2y + x = +8$

17) Through: $(1, 4)$, perpendecular to $y = -x + \frac{1}{2}$

18) Through: $(-3, 3)$, perpendecular to $y + 3x - 3 = 0$

Quadratic Equations - Square Roots Law

Solve each equation by taking square roots.

1) $x^2 + 8 = 8$

2) $x^2 + 8 = 44$

3) $18x^2 - 6 = 304$

4) $-10x^2 - 20 = -660$

5) $12x^2 + 6 = 978$

6) $15x^2 + 27 = 42$

7) $16x^2 - 34 = 4,942$

8) $14x^2 + 32 = 4,302$

9) $50x^2 = 2$

10) $2x^2 - 4 = 34$

11) $18x^2 - 10 = 1,214$

12) $4x^2 - 4 = 12$

13) $26x^2 - 6 = 8,418$

14) $26x^2 - 16 = -2,278$

15) $8x^2 - 8 = 24$

16) $27x^2 = 3$

17) $-16x^2 - 16 = -62$

18) $3x^2 - 6 = 51$

19) $21x^2 = -63$

20) $32x^2 = 98$

21) $4x^2 + 32 = 320$

22) $26x^2 = 234$

23) $-8x^2 + 6 = 170$

24) $2x^2 - 10 = -8$

25) $3x^2 - 15 = -12$

26) $4x^2 + 20 = 420$

27) $18x^2 + 2 = 650$

28) $14x^2 + 2 = 58$

Quadratic Equations - Factoring

Solve each equation by factoring.

1) $(6n - 4)(8n + 2) = 0$

2) $(15n - 3)(3n + 3) = 0$

3) $x^2 + 24 = 11x$

4) $14x^2 - 84 = -70x$

5) $20x^2 - 70 = 130x$

6) $14x^2 + 64 = 14 - 80x$

7) $-3x^2 + x + 72 = 3x^2 + 7x$

8) $16x^2 + 6x + 4 = 14x^2$

9) $32x^2 - 228x = -28$

10) $14x^2 + 64 = 14 - 80x$

11) $n(n - 5) = 0$

12) $(n + 2)(3n - 4) = 0$

13) $2x^2 = -36 - 18x$

14) $2x^2 = -8x - 8$

15) $x^2 = -6x - 9$

16) $2x^2 + 2x = 4$

17) $6x^2 - 16x = 32$

18) $x^2 = -12x - 36$

19) $9x^2 - 24x = 48$

20) $x^2 = -10x - 25$

21) $12x^2 - 32x = 64$

22) $6x^2 + 6x = 12$

23) $x^2 = -8x - 16$

24) $n(8n + 16) = 0$

Quadratic Equations - Completing the Square

Solve each equation by completing the square.

1) $2x^2 - 4x - 6 = 0$

2) $x^2 - 2x - 3 = 0$

3) $x^2 + \frac{5x}{4} - \frac{3}{2} = 0$

4) $-6x^2 + 4x + 16 = 0$

5) $2x^2 + 28x - 102 = 0$

6) $2x^2 + 12x + 16 = 0$

7) $2x^2 + 28x - 30 = 0$

8) $2x^2 - 8x - 182 = 14$

9) $3x^2 - 18x = -273$

10) $10x^2 = -40x + 120$

11) $4x^2 = 16x - 12$

12) $\frac{1}{3}x^2 - \frac{2}{3}x - 1 = 0$

13) $x^2 - 12x + 11 = 0$

14) $2x^2 - 20x + 52 = 16$

15) $2x^2 + 12x - 118 = 0$

16) $2x^2 = 36x + 80$

17) $2x^2 + 4x = -40$

18) $3x^2 - 36x + 33 = 0$

19) $4x^2 - 8x - 12 = 0$

20) $4x^2 + 56x - 60 = 0$

21) $3x^2 - 6x - 9 = 0$

22) $6x^2 = 24x - 18$

23) $-5x^2 - 30x - 40 = 0$

24) $-4x^2 - 24x - 32 = 0$

Quadratic Equations - Quadratic Formula

Solve each equation with the quadratic formula.

1) $2x^2 + 4x - 16 = 0$

2) $6x^2 = 12x - 6$

3) $2x^2 = 18x - 40$

4) $2x^2 + 10x - 12 = 0$

5) $10x^2 = 90x - 200$

6) $6x^2 - 24x - 86 = -14$

7) $6x^2 = -18x + 240$

8) $4x^2 + 20x - 24 = 0$

9) $8x^2 + 8x - 16 = 2$

10) $16x^2 - 8x = 36$

11) $2x^2 = -6x + 80$

12) $16x^2 - 32 = 4x$

13) $24x^2 + 18x = -15$

14) $4x^2 - x = \frac{15}{2}$

15) $4x^2 - 2x - 8 = 4$

16) $5x^2 = 45x - 100$

17) $4x^2 = -12x + 160$

18) $8x^2 - 16 = x$

19) $16x^2 + 12x = -10$

20) $10x^2 - 5x - 65 = 10$

21) $9x^2 = 54x - 27$

22) $24x^2 + 2 = 12x^2 + 14x$

23) $20x^2 + 18 = 2x$

24) $6x^2 - 3x - 12 = 6$

Arithmetic Sequences

Find the three terms in the sequence after the last one given.

1) $1, 4, 7, 10, ..., ..., ...,$

2) $-7, -9, -11, -13, ..., ..., ...,$

3) $a_1 = -26, d = 20$

4) $a_1 = -8.4, d = 0.8$

5) $a_{18} = 24.2, d = 1.1$

6) $a_n = (2n)^2$

7) $45, 42, 39, 36, ..., ..., ...,$

8) $-20, -30, -40, -50, ..., ..., ...,$

9) $a_n = -10 + 6n$, find a_{34}

10) $a_n = -3.1 - 2.1n$, find a_{12}

11) $a_5 = \frac{2}{5}, d = -\frac{1}{2}$

12) $a_n = \frac{n^2}{2n+1}$

13) $-15, -27, -39, ..., ..., ...,$

14) $a_n = 3n + 5$

15) $3, 8, 13, 18, ..., ..., ...,$

16) $-7, 2, 11, 20, ..., ..., ...,$

17) $\frac{3}{5}, \frac{4}{15}, -\frac{1}{15}, -\frac{2}{5}, ..., ..., ...,$

18) $2, -2, -6, ..., ..., ...,$

19) $7, 11, 15, ..., ..., ...,$

20) $10, 19, 28, ..., ..., ...,$

21) $-7.4, -6.5, -5.6, ..., ..., ...,$

22) $174, 374, 574, 774, ..., ..., ...,$

23) $-\frac{1}{5}, \frac{1}{20}, \frac{3}{10}, ..., ..., ...,$

24) $-1.75, -1.90, -2.05, ..., ..., ...,$

Geometric Sequences

Find the three terms in the sequence after the last one given.

1) $4, 8, 16, 32, .., ..., ...$

13) $a_n = -(-6)^{2n-1}$

2) $10, 5, 2.5, .., ..., ...$

14) $a_n = 3 \times (3)^{n-1} \ find \ a_4$

3) $a_n = a_1 \times 3, a_1 = 2$

15) $a_n = 2 \times (4)^{n-1} ; a_5 = ?$

4) $a_n = a_1 \times 5, a_1 = 1$

16) $2, \frac{1}{2}, \frac{1}{8}, ..., ..., ..., ...$

5) $0.8, -4, 20, -100 ..., ..., ...$

17) $2, 10, 50, ..., ..., ...$

6) $a_n = 3^{n-1}, a_1 = 1$

18) $8, -8, 8, ..., ..., ...$

7) $a_n = 4(\frac{1}{2})^{n-1}, a_1 = 2$

19) $486, 324, 216, ..., ..., ...$

8) $1, \frac{1}{3}, \frac{1}{9}, \frac{1}{27}, ..., ..., ...$

20) $-2.5, -7.5, -22.5, ..., ..., ...$

9) $a_n = 4a_1, a_1 = 3$

21) $-0.5, 2, -8, ..., ..., ...$

10) $1, 6, 36, ..., ..., ...$

22) $1, -7, 49, ..., ..., ...$

11) $-3, -6, -12, ..., ..., ...$

23) $a_n = -0.2(-5)^{n-1}$

12) $-1, -4, -16, ..., ..., ...$

24) $a_n = -4 \times 3^{n-1}$

Answer key Chapter 8

Relation and Functions

1) No, $D_f = \{7, -1, 12, -6, 8\}$, $R_f = \{0, 3, 5, -4, 13\}$

2) Yes, $D_f = \{3, 6, -1, 4, -3\}$, $R_f = \{3, 0, -1, 1\}$

3) Yes, $D_f = (-\infty, \infty)$, $R_f = \{-2, \infty)$

4) No, $D_f = \{1, 2, 4, 3, 2\}$, $R_f = \{-1, -3, 4, 0, 5\}$

5) No, $D_f = [-3, 2]$, $R_f = [-2, 3]$

6) Yes, $D_f = \{4, 1, 0, -2\}$, $R_f = \{0, 3, -2, 7\}$

Slope form

1) $y = -\frac{2}{3}x + 4$

2) $y = -\frac{1}{10}x + \frac{1}{2}$

3) $y = -2x - 3$

4) $y = \frac{6}{5}x - 2\frac{2}{5}$

5) $y = \frac{3}{2}x - \frac{21}{2}$

6) $y = 7x + 2$

7) $y = -x$

8) $y = \frac{10}{11}x + \frac{8}{11}$

9) $y = 0.5x + 2$

10) $y = 8x + 12$

11) $y = -10x - 15$

12) $y = -\frac{1}{12}x - \frac{3}{4}$

13) $y = 0.5x - 1$

14) $y = -4x + 20$

Slope and Y-Intercept

1) $m = \frac{1}{7}, b = 1$

2) $m = 5, b = 6$

3) $m = \frac{1}{2}, b = -3$

4) $m = 4, b = 32$

5) $m = 0, b = 5$

6) $m = -1, b = 1$

7) $m = undefind$, $b: no\ intercept$

8) $m = 3, b = 0$

9) $m = 3, b = 5$

10) $m = -\frac{7}{4}, b = -\frac{7}{24}$

Slope and One Point

1) $y = -x + 1$

2) $y = 4x - 1$

3) $y = -x - 10$

4) $y = 2x - 8$

5) $y = 7x - 5$

6) $y = \frac{5}{2}x + 4$

7) $y = -2$

8) $y = x - 1$

9) $y = 2x + 3$

10) $y = \frac{2}{5}x - \frac{2}{5}$

11) $y = -4x - 6$

12) $y = -x + 1$

13) $y = 3x - 4$

14) $x = 3$

15) $y = -\frac{1}{6}x + 4$

16) $y = \frac{1}{6}x + \frac{1}{6}$

17) $y = -9x + 31$

18) $y = 4x - 1$

19) $y = \frac{1}{2}x + 1$

20) $y = -\frac{3}{7}x - \frac{11}{7}$

21) $y = \frac{1}{2}x$

22) $y = -2x + 1$

23) $y = -2$

24) $y = -\frac{3}{4}x + \frac{1}{2}$

25) $y = 0$

26) $x = -4$

Slope of Two Points

1) $y = \frac{3}{2}x$

2) $y = 2x - 2$

3) $y = x + 3$

4) $y = \frac{-3}{2}x - \frac{9}{2}$

5) $y = 0$

6) $y = -x - 5$

7) $y = -2x + 10$

8) $y = -\frac{1}{2}x + 2$

9) $y = x - 3$

10) $x = 8$

11) $y = -\frac{2}{3}x + 4\frac{1}{3}$

12) $y = -3$

13) $y = -\frac{3}{10}x + 2\frac{1}{5}$

14) $y = \frac{4}{5}x - 2$

15) $y = x + 11$

16) $y = \frac{-1}{2}x + 5\frac{1}{2}$

17) $y = -x - 1$

18) $y = \frac{-7}{6}x - 5\frac{5}{6}$

19) $y = \frac{1}{2}x - 1$

20) $y = 2x + 2$

21) $y = -4x + 18$

22) $y = x + 5$

23) $y = -x + 4$

24) $y = -2x + 4$

Equation of Parallel and Perpendicular lines

1) $y = x$

2) $x = 5$

3) $y = -7x - 1$

4) $y = -6x + 21$

5) $y = \frac{5}{9}x + 3\frac{5}{9}$

6) $y = 9x - 26$

7) $y = \frac{1}{2}x + 1$

8) $y = 4x + 13$

9) $y = -x + 5$

10) $y = \frac{1}{4}x - 3$

11) $y = -3$

12) $y = -\frac{2}{3}x + 3$

13) $y = x - 1$

14) $y = \frac{1}{4}x + 1$

15) $y = -\frac{1}{2}x$

16) $y = -\frac{1}{2}x + 6$

17) $y = x + 3$

18) $y = \frac{1}{3}x + 4$

Quadratic Equations - Square Roots Law

1) 0

2) $\{6, -6\}$

3) $\{\frac{\sqrt{155}}{3}, -\frac{\sqrt{155}}{3}\}$

4) $\{8, -8\}$

5) $\{9, -9\}$

6) $\{1, -1\}$

7) $\{\sqrt{311}, -\sqrt{311}\}$

8) $\{\sqrt{305}, -\sqrt{305}\}$

9) $\{\frac{1}{5}, -\frac{1}{5}\}$

10) $\{\sqrt{19}, -\sqrt{19}\}$

11) $\{2\sqrt{17}, -2\sqrt{17}\}$

12) $\{2, -2\}$

13) $\{18, -18\}$

14) $\{i\sqrt{87}, -i\sqrt{87}\}$

15) $\{2, -2\}$

16) $\{\frac{1}{3}, -\frac{1}{3}\}$

17) $\{\frac{\sqrt{46}}{4}, -\frac{\sqrt{46}}{4}\}$

18) $\{\sqrt{19}, -\sqrt{19}\}$

19) $\{i\sqrt{3}, -i\sqrt{3}\}$

20) $\{\frac{7}{4}, -\frac{7}{4}\}$

21) $\{6\sqrt{2}, -6\sqrt{2}\}$

22) $\{3, -3\}$

23) $\{i\sqrt{\frac{41}{2}}, -i\sqrt{\frac{41}{2}}\}$

24) $\{1, -1\}$　　　　26) $\{10, -10\}$　　　　28) $\{2, -2\}$

25) $\{1, -1\}$　　　　27) $\{6, -6\}$

Quadratic Equations - Factoring

1) $\{\frac{2}{3}, -\frac{1}{4}\}$

2) $\{\frac{1}{5}, -1\}$

3) $\{3, 8\}$

4) $\{-6, 1\}$

5) $\{-\frac{1}{2}, 7\}$

6) $\{-\frac{5}{7}, -5\}$

7) $\{3. -4\}$

8) $\{-2, -1\}$

9) $\{\frac{1}{8}, 7\}$

10) $\{-\frac{5}{7}, -5\}$

11) $\{5, 0\}$

12) $\{-2, \frac{4}{3}\}$

13) $\{-6, -3\}$

14) $\{-2\}$

15) $\{-3\}$

16) $\{-2, 1\}$

17) $\{-\frac{4}{3}, 4\}$

18) $\{-6\}$

19) $\{-\frac{4}{3}, 4\}$

20) $\{-5\}$

21) $\{-\frac{4}{3}, 4\}$

22) $\{-2, 1\}$

23) $\{-4\}$

24) $\{-2, 0\}$

Quadratic Equations - Completing the Square

1) $\{-1, 3\}$

2) $\{3, -1\}$

3) $\{-2, \frac{3}{4}\}$

4) $\{2, -\frac{4}{3}\}$

5) $\{-17, 3\}$

6) $\{-2, -4\}$

7) $\{-15, 1\}$

8) $\{2 + \sqrt{102}, 2 - \sqrt{102}\}$

9) $\{3 + i\sqrt{82}, 3 - \sqrt{82}\}$

10) $\{-6, 2\}$

11) $\{3, 1\}$

12) $\{-1, 3\}$

13) $\{11, 1\}$

14) $\{5 + \sqrt{7}, 5 - \sqrt{7}\}$

15) $\{-3 + 2\sqrt{17}, -3 - 2\sqrt{17}\}$

16) $\{-2, 20\}$

17) $\{-1 + i\sqrt{19}, -1 - i\sqrt{19}\}$

18) $\{11, 1\}$

19) $\{3, -1\}$

20) $\{-15, 1\}$

21) $\{-1, 3\}$

22) $\{3, 1\}$

23) $\{-2, -4\}$

24) $\{-2, -4\}$

Quadratic Equations - Quadratic Formula

1) $\{2, -4\}$

2) $\{1\}$

3) $\{5, 4\}$

4) $\{1, -6\}$

5) $\{5, 4\}$

6) $\{6, -2\}$

7) $\{5, -8\}$

8) $\{1, -6\}$

9) $\{\frac{-1 + \sqrt{10}}{2}, \frac{-1 - \sqrt{10}}{2}\}$

10) $\{\frac{1 + \sqrt{37}}{4}, \frac{1 - \sqrt{37}}{4}\}$

11) $\{5, -8\}$

12) $\{\frac{1 + \sqrt{129}}{8}, \frac{1 - \sqrt{129}}{8}\}$

13) $\{\frac{-3 + i\sqrt{31}}{8}, \frac{-3 - i\sqrt{31}}{8}\}$

14) $\{\frac{3}{2}, -\frac{5}{4}\}$

15) $\{2, -\frac{3}{2}\}$

16) $\{5, 4\}$

17) $\{5, -8\}$

18) $\{\frac{1 + 3\sqrt{57}}{16}, \frac{1 - 3\sqrt{57}}{16}\}$

19) $\{\frac{-3 + i\sqrt{31}}{8}, \frac{-3 - i\sqrt{31}}{8}\}$

20) $\{3, -\frac{5}{2}\}$

21) $\{3+\sqrt{6}, 3-\sqrt{6}\}$

23) $\{\frac{1+i\sqrt{359}}{20}, \frac{1-i\sqrt{359}}{20}\}$

24) $\{2, -\frac{3}{2}\}$

22) $\{1, \frac{1}{6}\}$

Arithmetic sequences

1) $1, 4, 7, 10, 13, 16, 19$

2) $-7, -9, -11, -13, -15, -17, -19$

3) $-26, -6, 14, 34$

4) $-8.4, -7.6, -6.8, -6$

5) $5.5, 6.6, 7.7, 8.8$

6) $4, 16, 36$

7) $45, 42, 39, 36, 33, 30, 27$

8) $-20, -30, -40, -50, -60, -70, -80$

9) 194

10) -28.3

11) $\frac{12}{5}, \frac{19}{10}, \frac{7}{5}$

12) $\frac{1}{3}, \frac{4}{5}, \frac{9}{7}, \frac{16}{9}$

13) $-15, -27, -39, -51, -63, -75$

14) $8, 11, 14, 17$

15) $3, 8, 13, 18, 23., 28, 33$

16) $-7, 2, 11, 20, 29, 38, 47$

17) $\frac{3}{5}, \frac{4}{15}, -\frac{1}{15}, -\frac{2}{5}, -\frac{11}{15}, -\frac{16}{15}, -\frac{7}{5}$

18) $2, -2, -6, -10, -14, -18$

19) $7, 11, 15, 19, 23, 27$

20) $10, 19, 28, 37, 46, 55$

21) $-7.4, -6.5, -5.6, -4.7, -3.8, -2.9$

22) $174, 374, 574, 774, 974, 1174, 1374$

23) $\frac{11}{20}, \frac{4}{5}, \frac{21}{20}$

24) $-2.2, -2.35, -2.5$

Geometric sequences

1) $4, 8, 16, 32, 64, 128, 256$

2) $10, 5, 2.5, 1.25, 0.625, 0.3125$

3) $2, 6, 18, 54, 162$

4) $5, 25, 125, 625$

5) $0.8, -4, 20, -100, 500, -2,500, 12,500$

6) $1, 3, 9, 27$

7) $2, 1, \frac{1}{2}, \frac{1}{4}$

8) $\frac{1}{81}, \frac{1}{243}, \frac{1}{729}$

9) $3, 12, 48, 192$

10) $1, 6, 36, 216, 1296, 7776$

11) $-3, -6, -12, -24, -48, -96$

12) $-1, -4, -16, -64, -256, -1024$

13) $6, 216, 7776$

14) 81

15) 512

16) $2, \frac{1}{2}, \frac{1}{8}, \frac{1}{32}, \frac{1}{128}, \frac{1}{512}$

17) $2, 10, 50, 250, 1250, 6250$

18) $8, -8, 8, -8, 8, -8$

19) $486, 324, 216, 144, 96, 64$

20) $-2.5, -7.5, -22.5, -67.5, -202.5, -607.5$

21) $-0.5, 2, -8, 32, -128, 512$

22) $1, -7, 49, -343, 2401, -16807$

23) $-0.2, 1, -5$

24) $-4, -12, -36$

Chapter 9:

Geometry

Area and Perimeter of Square

Find the perimeter and area of each squares.

1)

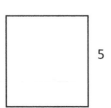

Perimeter:_____.

Area:_____.

2)

Perimeter:_____:

Area:_____:

3)

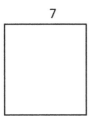

Perimeter:_____.

Area:_____.

4)

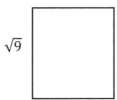

Perimeter:_____:

Area:_____:

5)

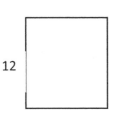

Perimeter:_____:

Area:_____:

6)

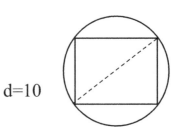

Perimeter of Square:_____:

Area of Square:_____:

Area and Perimeter of Rectangle

Find the perimeter and area of each rectangle.

1)

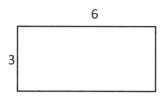

Perimeter:_____:

Area:_____:

2)

Perimeter:_____:

Area:_____:

3)

Perimeter:_____:

Area:_____:

4)

Perimeter:_____:

Area:_____:

5)

Perimeter:_____:

Area:_____:

6)

Perimeter:_____:

Area:_____:

Area and Perimeter of Triangle

Find the perimeter and area of each triangle.

1)

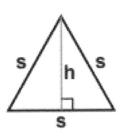

Perimeter:_____:

Area:_____:

2)

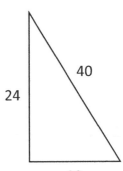

Perimeter:_____:

Area:_____:

3)

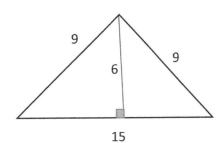

Perimeter:_____:

Area _____:

4)

s=8

h=6

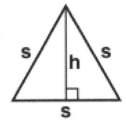

Perimeter:_____:

Area:_____:

5)

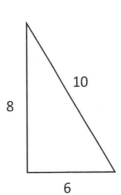

Perimeter:_____:

Area:_____:

6)

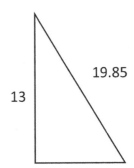

Perimeter:_____:

Area:_____:

Area and Perimeter of Trapezoid

Find the perimeter and area of each trapezoid.

1)

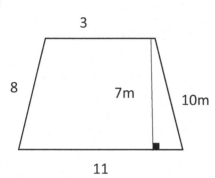

3

8   7m   10m

11

Perimeter:_____

Area:_____

2)

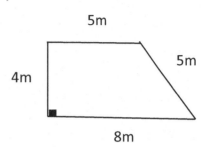

5m

4m   5m

8m

Perimeter:_____

Area:_____

3)

18

7   6

13

Perimeter:_____

Area   _____:

4)

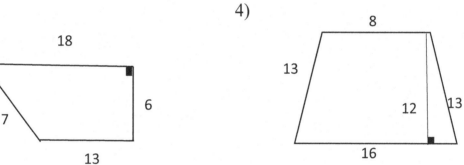

8

13   12   13

16

Perimeter:_____

Area:_____

5)

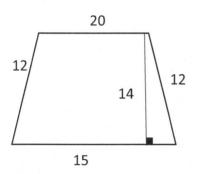

20

12   14   12

15

Perimeter:_____

Area:_____

6)

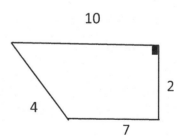

10

4   2

7

Perimeter:_____

Area:_____

Area and Perimeter of Parallelogram

Find the perimeter and area of each parallelogram.

1)

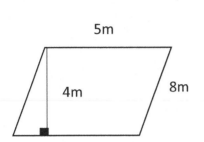

Perimeter:............

Area:............

2)

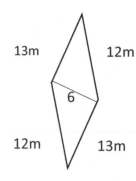

Perimeter:............

Area:............

3)

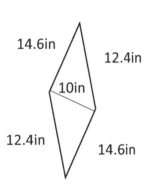

Perimeter:............

Area ....

4)

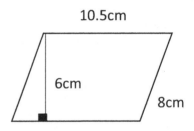

Perimeter:............

Area:............

5)

Perimeter:......

Area:............

6)

Perimeter:............

Area:............

Circumference and Area of Circle

Find the circumference and area of each ($\pi = 3.14$).

1)

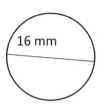

Circumference:

Area:

2)

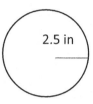

Circumference:_____.

Area:_____.

3)

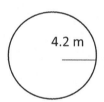

Circumference:_____.

Area _____.

4)

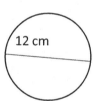

Circumference:_____.

Area:_____.

5)

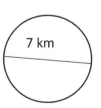

Circumference:_____.

Area:_____.

6)

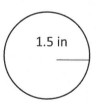

Circumference:_____.

Area:_____.

Perimeter of Polygon

Find the perimeter of each polygon.

1)

13mm

Perimeter:_____.

2)

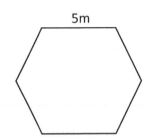

5m

Perimeter:_____:

3)

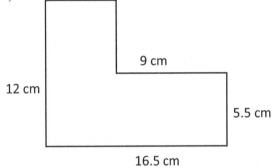

9 cm

12 cm

5.5 cm

16.5 cm

Perimeter:_____.

4)

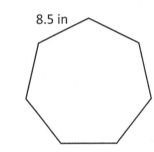

8.5 in

Perimeter:_____:

5)

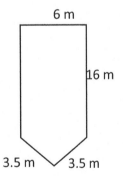

6 m

16 m

3.5 m   3.5 m

Perimeter:_____.

6)

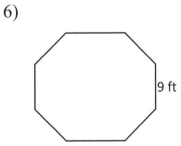

9 ft

Perimeter:_____:

Volume of Cubes

Find the volume of each cube.

1)

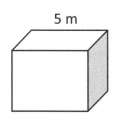

5 m

V:..

2)

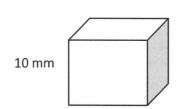

10 mm

V:..

3)

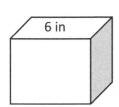

6 in

V:..

4)

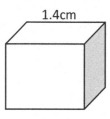

1.4cm

V:..

5)

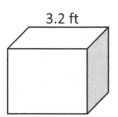

3.2 ft

V:..

6)

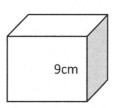

9cm

V:..

Volume of Rectangle Prism

Find the volume of each rectangle prism

1)

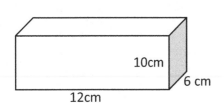

10cm
12cm
6 cm

V:................................:

2)

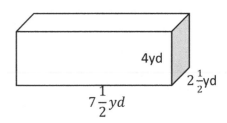

4yd
$7\frac{1}{2}yd$
$2\frac{1}{2}yd$

V:................................:

3)

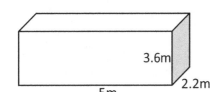

3.6m
5m
2.2m

V:................................:

4)

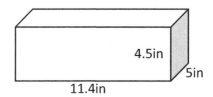

4.5in
11.4in
5in

V:................................:

5)

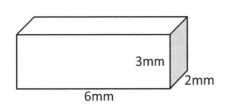

3mm
6mm
2mm

V:................................:

6)

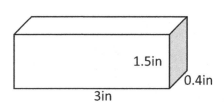

1.5in
3in
0.4in

V:................................:

Volume of Cylinder

Find the volume of each cylinder.

1)

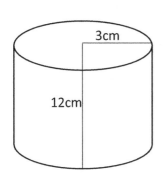

3cm

12cm

V:..

2)

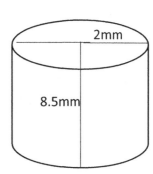

2mm

8.5mm

V:..

3)

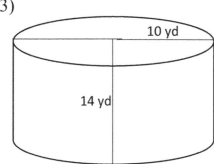

10 yd

14 yd

V:..

4)

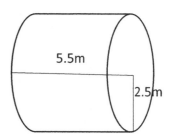

5.5m

2.5m

V:..

5)

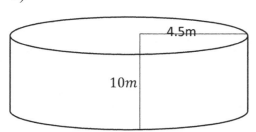

4.5m

10m

V:..

6)

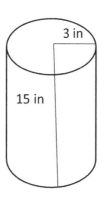

3 in

15 in

V:..

Volume of Spheres

Find the volume of each spheres ($\pi = 3.14$).

1)

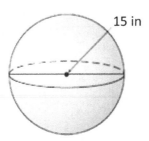

15 in

V:................................:

2)

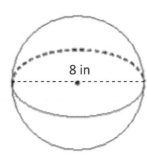

8 in

V:................................:

3)

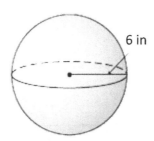

6 in

V:............................:

4)

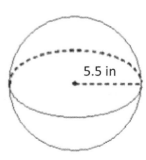

5.5 in

V:........................:

5)

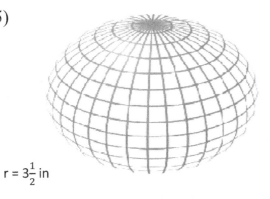

$r = 3\frac{1}{2}$ in

V:..............................:

6)

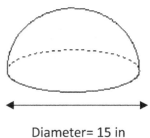

Diameter= 15 in

V:........................:

Volume of Pyramid and Cone

Find the volume of each pyramid and cone ($\pi = 3.14$).

1)

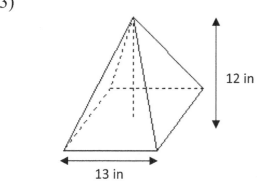

V:................................

2)

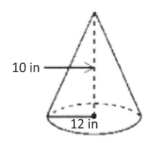

V:................................

3)

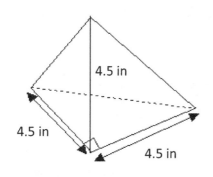

V:................................

4)

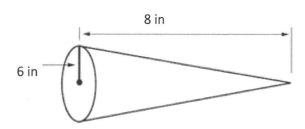

V:................................

5)

V:................................

6)

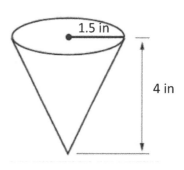

V:................................

Surface Area Cubes

Find the surface area of each cube.

1)

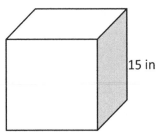

15 in

SA:_____.

2)

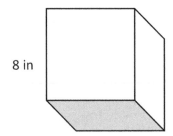

8 in

SA:_____.

3)

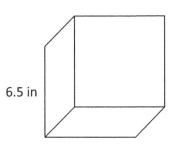

6.5 in

SA:_____.

4)

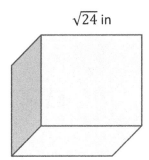

$\sqrt{24}$ in

SA:_____.

5)

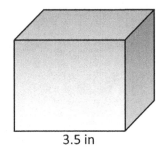

3.5 in

SA:_____.

6)

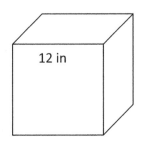

12 in

SA:_____.

Surface Area Rectangle Prism

Find the surface area of each rectangular prism.

1)

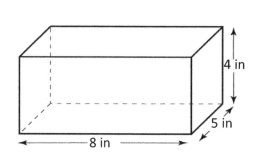

SA:................................:

2)

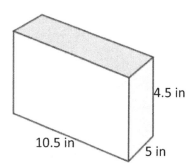

SA:................................:

3)

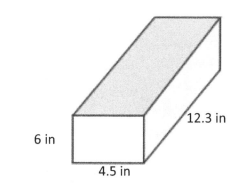

SA:................................:

4)

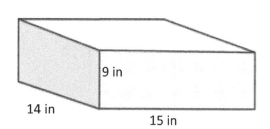

SA:................................:

5)

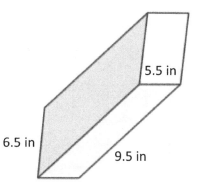

SA:................................:

6)

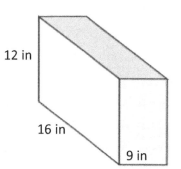

SA:................................:

Surface Area Cylinder

Find the surface area of each cylinder.

1)

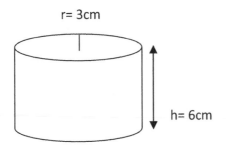

r= 3cm

h= 6cm

SA:_____.

2)

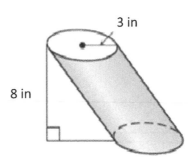

3 in

8 in

SA:_____.

3)

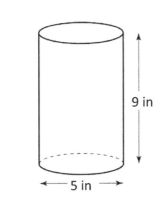

9 in

5 in

SA:_____.

4)

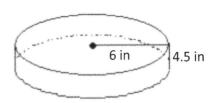

6 in   4.5 in

SA:_____.

5)

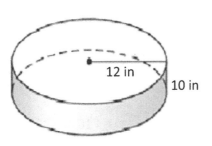

12 in

10 in

SA:_____.

6)

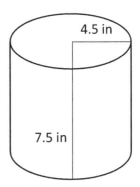

4.5 in

7.5 in

SA:_____.

Answer key Chapter 9

Area and Perimeter of Square

1. Perimeter: 20, Area:25
2. Perimeter: $4\sqrt{6}$, Area:6
3. Perimeter: 28, Area:49
4. Perimeter: $4\sqrt{9}$, Area:9
5. Perimeter: 48, Area:144
6. Perimeter: $4\sqrt{50}$, Area:50

Area and Perimeter of Rectangle

1- Perimeter: 18, Area:18
2- Perimeter: 40, Area:96
3- Perimeter: 50, Area:150
4- Perimeter: 19, Area: 17.5
5- Perimeter: 4.23, Area: 1
6- Perimeter: 14, Area:10

Area and Perimeter of Triangle

1- Perimeter: 3s, Area:$\frac{1}{2}sh$
2- Perimeter: 96, Area:384
3- Perimeter: 33, Area:45
4- Perimeter: 24, Area:24
5- Perimeter: 24, Area:24
6- Perimeter: 47.9, Area:97.5

Area and Perimeter of Trapezoid

1- Perimeter: 32, Area:49
2- Perimeter: 22, Area:26
3- Perimeter: 44, Area:93
4- Perimeter: 50, Area:144
5- Perimeter: 59, Area:245
6- Perimeter: 23, Area:17

Area and Perimeter of Parallelogram

1- Perimeter: $26m$, Area:$20(m)^2$
2- Perimeter: $50m$, Area:$78(m)^2$
3- Perimeter: $54in$, Area:$146(in)^2$
4- Perimeter: $37cm$, Area:$63(cm)^2$
5- Perimeter: $85m$, Area:$441(m)^2$
6- Perimeter: $48m$, Area:$144(m)^2$

Circumference and Area of Circle

1) Circumference:50.24 mm   Area:$200.96(mm)^2$
2) Circumference: 15.7in   Area:$(19.63in)^2$
3) Circumference: 26.38 m   Area:$55.39(m)^2$
4) Circumference: 37.68 cm   Area:113.04
5) Circumference: 21.98 in   Area:$38.47(in)^2$
6) Circumference: 9.42 km   Area:$7.07(km)^2$

Perimeter of Polygon

1) 65 mm
2) 30 m
3) 57 cm
4) 59.5 in
5) 45 m
6) 72 ft

Volume of Cubes

1) $125m^3$
2) $1{,}000(mm)^3$
3) $216in^3$
4) $2.74(cm)^3$

5) $32.77(ft)^3$ 6) $729(cm)^3$

Volume of Rectangle Prism

1) $720(cm)^3$ 3) $39.6(m)^3$ 5) $36(mm)^3$

2) $75(yd)^3$ 4) $256.5(in)^3$ 6) $1.8(in)^3$

Volume of Cylinder

1) $339.12(cm)^3$ 3) $1,099(yd)^3$ 5) $635.85(m)^3$

2) $26.69(mm)^3$ 4) $107.94(m)^3$ 6) $423.9(in)^3$

Volume of Spheres

1) $1,766.25(in)^3$ 3) $904.32(in)^3$ 5) $179.5(in)^3$

2) $267.95(in)^3$ 4) $696.56(in)^3$ 6) $883.13(in)^3$

Volume of Pyramid and Cone

1) $512 (in)^3$ 3) $676 (in)^3$ 5) $15.19 (in)^3$

2) $1507.2 (in)^3$ 4) $301.44 (in)^3$ 6) $9.42 (in)^3$

Surface Area Cubes

1) $1,350(in)^2$ 3) $253.5(in)^2$ 5) $73.5(in)^2$

2) $384(in)^2$ 4) $144(in)^2$ 6) $864(in)^2$

Surface Area Rectangle Prism

1) $184(in)^2$ 3) $312.3(in)^2$ 5) $299.5(in)^2$

2) $244.5(in)^2$ 4) $942(in)^2$ 6) $888(in)^2$

Surface Area Cylinder

1) $169.56(in)^2$ 3) $180.55(in)^2$ 5) $1,657.92(in)^2$

2) $207.24(in)^2$ 4) $395.64(in)^2$ 6) $339.12(in)^2$

Chapter 10: Statistics and probability

Mean, Median, Mode, and Range of the Given Data

Find the mean, median, mode(s), and range of the following data.

1) 26, 69, 30, 27, 19, 54, 27

Mean: __, Median: __, Mode: __, Range: __

2) 8, 12, 12, 15, 18, 20

Mean: __, Median: __, Mode: __, Range: __

3) 51, 32, 29, 33, 39, 17, 25, 29, 12

Mean: __, Median: __, Mode: __, Range: __

4) 10, 7, 3, 9, 2, 4

Mean: __, Median: __, Mode: __, Range: __

5) 20, 16, 10, 19, 13, 18, 12, 9, 9, 7

Mean: __, Median: __, Mode: __, Range: __

6) 9, 17, 18, 9, 6, 18, 8, 12

Mean: __, Median: __, Mode: __, Range: __

7) 49, 48, 86, 96, 34, 64, 48, 14, 32, 64

Mean: __, Median: __, Mode: __, Range: __

8) 45, 45, 47, 88, 89

Mean: __, Median: __, Mode: __, Range: __

9) 18, 18, 28, 36, 64

Mean: __, Median: __, Mode: __, Range: __

10) 10, 8, 2, 2, 5, 8, 1

Mean: __, Median: __, Mode: __, Range: __

11) 5, 9, 3, 5, 1, 7

Mean: __, Median: __, Mode: __, Range: __

12) 6, 7, 11, 11, 12, 12, 12

Mean: __, Median: __, Mode: __, Range: __

13) 8, 8, 0, 16, 0, 8, 16

Mean: __, Median: __, Mode: __, Range: __

14) 12, 18, 20, 7, 11, 10, 12, 16

Mean: __, Median: __, Mode: __, Range: __

15) 6, 12, 15, 15, 20

Mean: __, Median: __, Mode: __, Range: __

16) 9, 9, 12, 10, 12, 8, 17

Mean: __, Median: __, Mode: __, Range: __

17) 20, 8, 6, 9, 18, 19, 9, 6

Mean: __, Median: __, Mode: __, Range: __

18) 62, 16, 16, 28, 3, 2

Mean: __, Median: __, Mode: __, Range: __

19) 55, 22, 24, 55, 2, 4

Mean: __, Median: __, Mode: __, Range: __

20) 98, 64, 73, 86, 91, 98, 79

Mean: __, Median: __, Mode: __, Range: __

Box and Whisker Plot

1) Draw a box and whisker plot for the data set:

24, 21, 22, 26, 24, 22, 26, 26, 30

2) The box-and-whisker plot below represents the math test scores of 20 students.

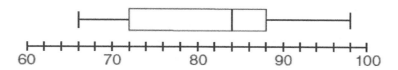

A. What percentage of the test scores are less than 72?

B. Which interval contains exactly 50% of the grades?

C. What is the range of the data?

D. What do the scores 66, 84, and 98 represent?

E. What is the value of the lower and the upper quartile?

F. What is the median score?

Bar Graph

Each student in class selected two games that they would like to play. Graph the given information as a bar graph and answer the questions below:

Game	Votes
Football	12
Volleyball	9
Basketball	15
Baseball	19
Tennis	15

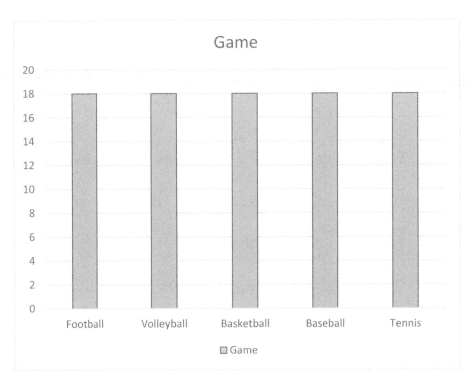

1) Which was the most popular game to play?

2) How many more student like Baseball than Football?

3) Which two game got the same number of votes?

4) How many Volleyball and Football did student vote in all?

5) Did more student like football or Tennis?

6) Which game did the fewest student like?

Histogram

Create a histogram for the set of data.

Math Test Score out of 100 points.

68	84	73	90	93	75	80	96	77	64
91	83	92	85	81	66	97	76	84	82
94	65	86	83	77	95	79	78	62	97

Frequency Table	
Interval	**Number of Values**

Dot plots

The ages of students in a Math class are given below.

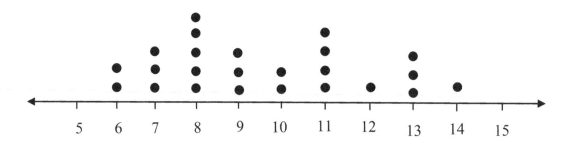

1) What is the total number of students in math class?

2) How many students are at least 11 years old?

3) Which age(s) has the most students?

4) Which age(s) has the fewest student?

5) Determine the median of the data.

6) Determine the range of the data.

7) Determine the mode of the data.

Scatter Plots

A person charges an hourly rate for his services based on the number of hours a

job takes.

Hours	Rate
1	$25
2	$22.50
3	$21.50
4	$20

Hours	Rate
5	$19.50
6	$18
7	$17.50
8	$17

1) Draw a scatter plot for this data.

2) Does the data have positive or negative correlation?

3) Sketch the line that best fits the data.

4) Find the slope of the line.

5) Write the equation of the line using slope-intercept form.

6) Using your prediction equation: If a job takes 10 hours, what would be the

   hourly rate?

Stem–And–Leaf Plot

Make stem-and-leaf plots for the given data.

1) 22, 26, 28, 21, 42, 24, 48, 47, 29, 24, 19, 12, 45

Stem	leaf

2) 52, 54, 27, 31, 52, 24, 36, 58, 38, 34, 39, 32

Stem	leaf

3) 113, 106, 95, 95, 100, 115, 92, 114, 98, 112, 96, 107

Stem	leaf

4) 22, 15, 27, 21, 79, 24, 70, 77, 29, 24, 19, 12

Stem	leaf

5) 66, 69, 123, 67, 19, 126, 120

Stem	leaf

6) 112, 87, 96, 85, 110, 117, 92, 114, 88, 112, 98, 90

Stem	leaf

Pie Graph

80 people were survey on their favorite ice cream. The pie graph is made according to their responses. Answer following questions based on the Pie graph.

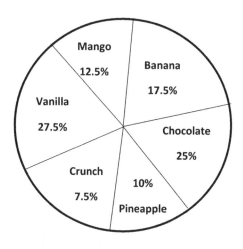

1) How many people like to eat Banana ice cream? _____

2) Approximately, which two ice creams did about half the people like the best? _____

3) How many people said either mango or crunch ice cream was their favorite? _____

4) How many people would like to have chocolate ice cream? _____

5) Which ice cream is the favorite choice of 22 people? _____

Probability

1) A jar contains 12 caramels, 7 mints and 16 dark chocolates. What is the probability of selecting a mint?

2) If you were to roll the dice one time what is the probability it will NOT land on a 2?

3) A die has sides are numbered 1 to 6. If the cube is thrown once, what is the probability of rolling a 6?

4) The sides of number cube have the numbers 3, 5, 7, 3, 5, and 7. If the cube is thrown once, what is the probability of rolling a 5?

5) Your friend asks you to think of a number from eight to twenty. What is the probability that his number will be 13?

6) A person has 5 coins in their pocket. A dime, 2 pennies, a quarter, and a nickel. If a person randomly picks one coin out of their pocket. What would the probability be that they get a penny?

7) What is the probability of drawing an odd numbered card from a standard deck of shuffled cards?

8) 24 students apply to go on a school trip. Three students are selected at random. what is the probability of selecting 3 students?

Answer key Chapter 10

Mean, Median, Mode, and Range of the Given Data

1) mean: 36, median: 27, mode: 27, range: 50

2) mean: 14.17, median: 13.5, mode: 12, range: 12

3) mean: 29.7, median: 29, mode: 29, range: 39

4) mean: 5.83, median: 5.5, mode No mode. range: 8

5) mean: 13.3, median: 12.5, mode: 9, range: 13

6) mean: 12.125, median: 10.5, mode: 9,18, range: 12

7) mean: 53.5, median: 48.5, mode: 48 and 64, range: 82

8) mean: 62.8, median: 47, mode: 45, range: 44

9) mean: 32.8, median: 28, mode: 18, range: 46

10) mean: 5.1, median: 5, mode: 2,8, range: 9

11) mean: 5, median: 5, mode: 5, range: 8

12) mean: 10.14, median: 11, mode: 12, range: 6

13) mean: 8, median: 8, mode: 8, range: 16

14) mean: 13.25, median: 12, mode: 12, range: 13

15) mean: 13.6, median: 15, mode: 15, range: 14

16) mean: 11, median: 10, mode: 9,12, range: 9

17) mean: 11.88, median: 9, mode: 6,9, range: 14

18) mean: 21.17, median: 16, mode: 16, range: 60

19) mean: 27, median: 23, mode: 55, range: 53

20) mean: 84.14, median: 86, mode: 98, range: 34

Box and Whisker Plot

1)

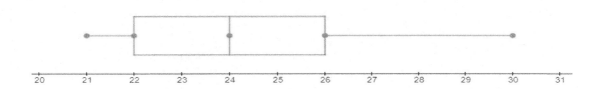

2)

A. 25%

C. 32

B. 72-84

D. Minimum, Median, and Maximum

E. Lower (Q_1) is 72 and upper (Q_3) is 88   F. 84

Bar Graph

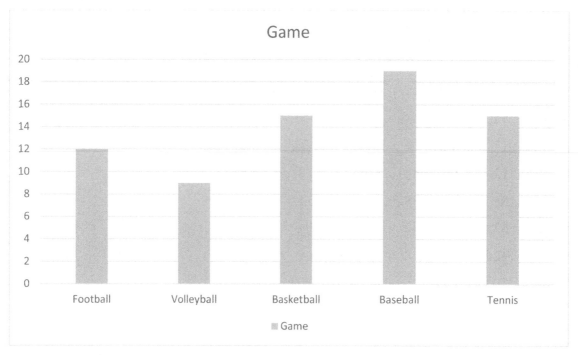

1) Baseball

2) 7 students

3) Basketball and Tennis

4) 21

5) Tennis

6) Volleyball

Histogram

Frequency Table	
Interval	**Number of Values**
62-67	4
68-73	2
74-79	6
80-85	8
86-91	3
92-97	7

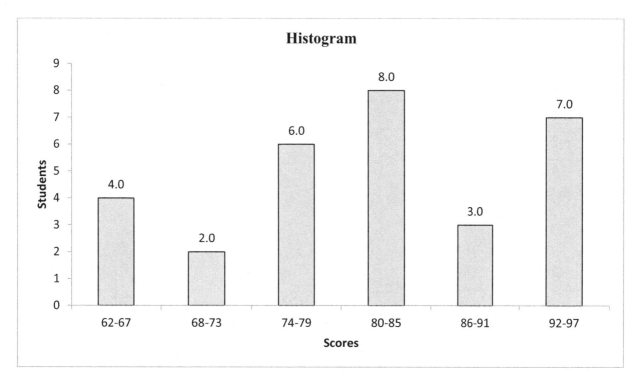

Dot plots

1) 24
2) 9
3) 8
4) 12 and 14

5) 3
6) 8
7) 3

Scatter Plots

1)

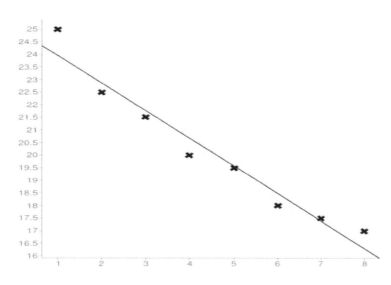

2) Negative correlation
3) ----
4) Slope(m)= -1

5) $y = -x + 25$
6) 15

Stem–And–Leaf Plot

1)

Stem	leaf
1	2 9
2	1 2 4 4 6 8 9
4	2 7 8 5

2)

Stem	leaf
2	4 7
3	1 2 4 6 8 9
5	2 2 4 8

3)

Stem	leaf
9	2 5 5 6 8
10	0 6 7
11	2 3 4 5

4)

Stem	leaf
1	2 9 5
2	1 2 4 4 7 9
7	0 7 9

5)

Stem	leaf
1	9
6	6 7 9
12	0 3 6

6)

Stem	leaf
8	5 7 8
9	0 2 6 8
11	0 2 2 4 7

Pie Graph

1) 14

2) Vanilla and chocolate

3) 16

4) 20

5) Vanilla

Probability

1) $\frac{1}{5}$

2) $\frac{5}{6}$

3) $\frac{1}{6}$

4) $\frac{1}{3}$

5) $\frac{1}{12}$

6) $\frac{2}{5}$

7) $\frac{4}{13}$

8) $\frac{1}{8}$

PERT Test Review

PERT Test Mathematics Formula Sheet

Area of a:	
Parallelogram	$A = bh$
Trapezoid	$A = \frac{1}{2}h(b_1 + b_2)$

Surface Area and Volume of a:		
Rectangular/Right Prism	$SA = ph + 2B$	$V = Bh$
Cylinder	$SA = 2\pi rh + 2\pi r^2$	$V = \pi r^2 h$
Pyramid	$SA = \frac{1}{2}ps + B$	$V = \frac{1}{3}Bh$
Cone	$SA = \pi rs + \pi r^2$	$V = \frac{1}{3}\pi r^2 h$
Sphere	$SA = 4\pi r^2$	$V = \frac{4}{3}\pi r^3$

(p = perimeter of base B; $\pi = 3.14$)

Algebra	
Slope of a line	$m = \dfrac{y_2 - y_1}{x_2 - x_1}$
Slope-intercept form of the equation of a line	$y = mx + b$
Point-slope form of the Equation of a line	$y - y_1 = m(x - x_1)$
Standard form of a Quadratic equation	$y = ax^2 + bx + c$
Quadratic formula	$x = \dfrac{-b \pm \sqrt{b^2 - 4ac}}{2a}$
Pythagorean theorem	$a^2 + b^2 = c^2$
Simple interest	

$$I = prt$$
(I = interest, p = principal, r = rate, t = time)

PERT Practice Test 1

Mathematics

Total Number of Questions: 30 Questions

Total time: No Limit Time.

Be sure to review each answer carefully before submitting. You will not be able to go back to any questions.

You will only have access to a calculator app provided at your testing station.

Administered *Month Year*

1) Arrange the following fractions in order from least to greatest.

$$\frac{3}{7}, \frac{5}{9}, \frac{1}{3}, \frac{19}{21}, \frac{11}{18}$$

A. $\frac{1}{3}, \frac{3}{7}, \frac{5}{9}, \frac{11}{18}, \frac{19}{21}$

B. $\frac{5}{9}, \frac{3}{7}, \frac{1}{3}, \frac{11}{18}, \frac{19}{21}$

C. $\frac{19}{21}, \frac{11}{18}, \frac{5}{9}, \frac{3}{7}, \frac{1}{3}$

D. $\frac{11}{18}, \frac{19}{21}, \frac{1}{3}, \frac{3}{7}, \frac{5}{9}$

2) Elena earn \$9.20 an hour and worked 35 hours. Her brother earns \$11.50 an hour. How many hours would her brother need to work to equal Elena's earnings over 40 hours?

A. 15.22

B. 28

C. 35

D. 80.50

3) In a library, 40% of the books are fiction and the rest are non-fiction. Given that there are 1,200 more non-fiction books than fiction books, what is the total number of books in the library?

A. 2,000

B. 5,000

C. 6,000

D. 4,000

4) Which of the following expressions is undefined in the set of real numbers?

A. $\sqrt[2]{148}$

B. $\sqrt[3]{-27}$

C. $\sqrt{-81}$

D. $\sqrt[4]{16}$

5) If $f(x) = 5x^2$, and 3f(2a) = 540 then what could be the value of a?

A. -3

B. -1

C. 1

D. 3

6) What is the value of 3^4?

A. $(3 + 3)^2$

B. 9^2

C. $3(3^2)$

D. $3^2 + 3^2$

7) Shane Williams puts $3,800 into a saving bank account that pays simple interest of 4.5%. How much interest will she earn after 3 years?

A. $5,130

B. $ 1,710

C. $513

D. $171

8) A map has the scale of 5 cm to 1 km. What is the actual area of a lake on ground which is represented as an area of 80 cm^2 on the map?

   A. 16 km^2

   B. 3.2 km^2

   C. 16 cm^2

   D. 3.2 cm^2

9) Which equation can be equal "4 more than the ratio of a number to 5 is equal to 7 less than the number"?

   A. $4x - 5 = 7 - x$

   B. $4 + \frac{x}{5} = x - 7$

   C. $\frac{4}{5}x - 7 = 5x$

   D. $4 + 5x = 7 - x$

10) Three angles join to form a straight angle. One angle measure 55°. Other angle measures 30°. What is the measure of third angle?

   A. 5°

   B. 15°

   C. 35°

   D. 95°

11) Evaluate $\frac{32x^5y^7z^{-2}}{12\,x^2y^9z^0}$.

    A. $\frac{4x^3y^2}{3\,z^2}$

    B. $\frac{4x^3z^2}{3\,y^2}$

    C. $\frac{8x^3}{3\,y^2z^2}$

    D. $\frac{8y^2}{3\,x^3z^2}$

12) Find the equation for line passing through $(2, -1)$ and $(4,2)$.

    A. $-3x - 2y = 10$

    B. $2y - 3x = -8$

    C. $-3x + 2y = 10$

    D. $2y + 3x = -8$

13) Which of the following equations best represents the line in the graph below?

    A. $y = \frac{1}{2}x + 2$

    B. $y = x + 5$

    C. $y = \frac{1}{2}x - 2$

    D. $y = x + 2$

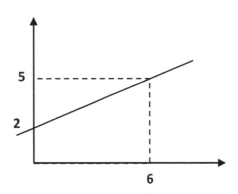

14) lengths of Two sides of a triangle are 5 and 8. Which of the following could

Not be the measure of third side?

A. 2

B. 4

C. 9

D. 11

15) Rosie is x years old. She is 3 years older than her twin brothers Milan and

Marcel. What is the mean age of the three children?

A. $x + 2$

B. $x - 3$

C. $x + 3$

D. $x - 2$

16) a is inversely proportional to $(2b - 5)$. If a = 15 and b = 7, express a in terms

of b.

A. $a = 2b - 5$

B. $a = 105(2b - 5)$

C. $a = \frac{135}{2b-5}$

D. $a = \frac{2b-5}{135}$

17) If $-3x + 4y = -5$ and $2x - 5y = 8$, what is the value of x?

    A. 2

    B. 2.60

    C. -8

    D. -1

18) Emma and Mia buy a total of 17 books. Emma bought 5 more books than Mia did. How many books did Emma buy?

    A. 7

    B. 11

    C. 12

    D. 15

19) The line n has a slope of $\frac{c}{d}$, where c and d are integers. What is the slope of a line that is perpendicular to line n?

    A. $\frac{c}{d}$

    B. $-\frac{c}{d}$

    C. $\frac{d}{c}$

    D. $-\frac{d}{c}$

20) For what value(s) of x is the following equation true: $3x^2 - 18x + 27 = 0$?

    A. $3, 6$

    B. $+3$

    C. -3

    D. ± 3

21) Solve the linear inequality: $-\dfrac{(5x-8)}{4} + 9 \geq 11$

    A. $x \leq 0$

    B. $x > 0$

    C. $x \geq 0$

    D. $x < 0$

22) Evaluate: $\dfrac{(x^2+5x+6)}{(2x^2-8x+8)} \div \dfrac{(x^2+2x-3)}{(x^2-3x+2)} = ?$

    A. $\dfrac{x+2}{2x-2}$

    B. $\dfrac{2(x+2)}{x-2}$

    C. $\dfrac{x-2}{2x-4}$

    D. $\dfrac{x+2}{x-2}$

23) 221 is What percent of 170?

    A. $130\,\%$

    B. $77\,\%$

    C. $30\,\%$

    D. $123\,\%$

24) Express as a single fraction in its simplest form: $\frac{5}{(x-2)} - \frac{6}{(3x+1)} = ?$

    A. $\frac{9x+17}{(x-2)(3x+1)}$

    B. $\frac{9x-17}{(x-2)(3x+1)}$

    C. $\frac{9x+17}{3x-2}$

    D. $\frac{-1}{3x-2}$

25) Ryan is x years old and her sister Mitzi is $(5x - 18)$ years old. Given that Mitzi is twice as old as Ryan, what is Mitzi's age?

    A. 6

    B. 9

    C. 12

    D. 18

26) The set of possible values of p is $\{2,5,11\}$. What is the set of possible values of h if $3h = 2p + 2$?

    A. $\{2,5,11\}$

    B. $\{6,15,33\}$

    C. $\{2,4,8\}$

    D. $\{6,12,24\}$

27) In the infinitely repeating decimal below, 1 is the first digit in the repeating pattern. What is the 391st digit? $\frac{1}{7} = \overline{0.142857}$

   A. 1

   B. 4

   C. 8

   D. 5

28) Consider the following series: 7, 5, 2, 9, 14, 16. What number should come next?

   A. 18

   B. 21

   C. 25

   D. 30

29) Evaluate: $(3y - x)(x - 2y)$?

   A. $-x^2 - 2xy + 6y^2$

   B. $x^2 - 5xy + 6y^2$

   C. $-x^2 + 5xy - 6y^2$

   D. $-x^2 + xy - 6y^2$

30) A cube has a side length of 140 cm, what is its volume in cubic meters?

   $(100\ cm = 1\ m)$

   A. 4.20

   B. 1.96

   C. 2.80

   D. 2.744

"End of PERT Practice Test 1"

PERT Practice Test 2

Mathematics

Total Number of Questions: 30 Questions

Total time: No Limit Time.

Be sure to review each answer carefully before submitting. You will not be able to go back to any questions.

You will only have access to a calculator app provided at your testing station.

Administered *Month Year*

1) What is the sum of the smallest prime number and three times the largest negative even integer?

    A. -2

    B. 0

    C. -4

    D. -6

2) What is the number a, if the result of adding a to 42 is the same as subtracting $3a$ from 230?

    A. -94

    B. 68

    C. 188

    D. 47

3) Solve these fractions and reduce to its simplest terms: $4\frac{1}{21} - 5\frac{4}{7} + 2\frac{1}{3} =$

    A. $\frac{17}{21}$

    B. $-1\frac{4}{21}$

    C. $\frac{6}{7}$

    D. $1\frac{2}{3}$

4) Find the solution set of the following equation: $|2x - 3| = 5$

A. $\{4, -1\}$

B. $\{1, -1\}$

C. $\{5\}$

D. $\{-4, 1\}$

5) What is the solution to the pair of equations below? $\begin{cases} x - 3y = 1 \\ 2x + y = 2 \end{cases}$

A. $x = 4$ and $y = 1$

B. $x = 0$ and $y = 1$

C. $x = 1$ and $y = 0$

D. $x = 1$ and $y = -3$

6) What is $\sqrt[4]{4^{-8}}$ in simplest form?

A. $\dfrac{1}{65,536}$

B. $\dfrac{1}{256}$

C. $\dfrac{1}{64}$

D. $\dfrac{1}{16}$

7) What is 3.21×10^{-4} in standard form?

A. $-32,120$

B. -0.000321

C. $\dfrac{1}{32,100}$

D. 0.000321

8) What is the value of x in the triangle?

   A. 77°

   B. 130°

   C. 50°

   D. 103°

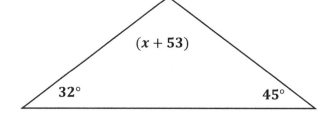

9) Find the length of the unknown side.

   A. 23.3 ft

   B. 16 ft

   C. 256 ft

   D. 8 ft

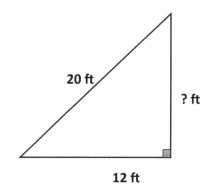

10) A store sells all of its products at a price 18% greater than the price the store paid for the product. How much does the store sell a product if the store paid $250 for it?

   A. $268

   B. $205

   C. $295

   D. $45

11) Which statement correctly describes the value of N in the equation below?

$$4(7N - 12) = 7(4N - 12)$$

A. N has no correct solutions.

B. N=0 is one solution.

C. N has infinitely many correct solutions.

D. N=1 is one solution.

12) What is the probability of Not spinning at F?

A. $\frac{5}{8}$

B. $\frac{3}{8}$

C. $\frac{1}{3}$

D. $\frac{1}{5}$

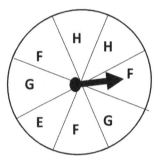

13) A position of subway station and Grace's house shown by a grid. The station is located at $(-2, -7)$, and her house is located at $(6, -1)$. What is the distance between her house and the subway stop?

A. 8

B. 10

C. $8\sqrt{2}$

D. 6

14) What is solution to the equation $\sqrt{3x - 1} = 4$?

    A. -1

    B. -5

    C. 1

    D. 5

15) The equation $x = 2y - 4$ has a y-intercept of?

    A. 2

    B. -4

    C. $\frac{1}{2}$

    D. $-\frac{1}{4}$

16) If $3^{2x} = 81$, then $x = ?$

    A. 4

    B. 3

    C. 2

    D. 1

17) Which is the value of x^2, if $x^2 + x = 30$?

    A. 16

    B. -25

    C. 30

    D. 36

18) Each of 5 pitchers can contain up to $\frac{3}{5}$ L of water. If each of the pitcher is at least the half full, which of the following expressions represents the total amount of water, W, contained on all 5 pitchers?

A. $0.6 < w < 6$

B. $0 < w < 1.5$

C. $0 < w < 3$

D. $1.5 < w < 3$

19) What is the simplest form of the expression $\frac{2x^2-7x-4}{4(x^2-\frac{1}{4})}$?

A. $\frac{x+4}{4(x-\frac{1}{2})}$

B. $\frac{x-4}{2x-1}$

C. $\frac{x+4}{2x+1}$

D. $\frac{2x-1}{x-4}$

20) What is the simplest form of the expression $\frac{(5x^{-2}y^3)^2}{125y^{-2}z^{-1}}$, (using positive exponent)?

A. $\frac{2y^8z^2}{25x^4}$

B. $\frac{y^8z}{5x^4}$

C. $\frac{2x^4}{25zy^8}$

D. $\frac{x^4}{5y^8z}$

21) The line $2y - 1 = 4x + 5$ and $4y - 1 = 2x + 5$ are

   A. Parallel

   B. Perpendicular

   C. The same line

   D. Neither parallel nor perpendicular

22) Find the slope of the line.

   A. $\dfrac{1}{2}$

   B. $\dfrac{1}{3}$

   C. 2

   D. $-\dfrac{1}{2}$

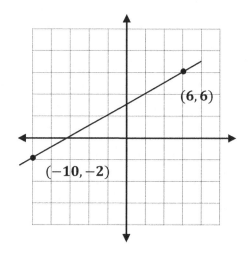

(6, 6)

(−10, −2)

23) Let $f(x) = 5x - 2$. If $f(a) = -12$ and $f(b) = 13$, then what is $f(a + b)$?

   A. -2

   B. 2

   C. 3

   D. -3

24) if $xy - 5x = 32$ and $y - 5 = 8$, then $x = ?$

   A. 32

   B. 16

   C. 8

   D. 4

25) What is the number of sides of a regular polygon whose interior angles are 144° each? (Remember, the sum of exterior angles of any polygon is 360°).

   A. 5

   B. 10

   C. 6

   D. 12

26) The sum of two consecutive integers is −15. If 1 is added to the smaller integer and 2 is subtracted from the larger integer, what is the product of the two resulting integers?

   A. 63

   B. 60

   C. 56

   D. 72

27) $3 + (5n + 8) - (6n + 5)$

   A. $6 - n$

   B. $6 + n$

   C. $16 - n$

   D. $16 + n$

28) If the line m is parallel to the side BC of ABC, what is angle n?

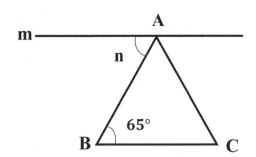

    A. 115

    B. 65

    C. 25

    D. 15

29) The operation is defined as $a @ b = a - 2ab$

    The operation # is defined as $a\#b = 2a - b^2$

    If $f(x) = -x^2 - 4$, what is the value of $\big(f(-1)@f(2)\big)\#f(3)$?

    A. -62

    B. -35

    C. -235

    D. 165

30) What is the percent equivalent of 0.004?

    A. 40%

    B. 4%

    C. 0.40%

    D. 0.04%

"End of PERT Practice Test 2"

Answers and

Explanations

Answer Key

Now, it's time to review your results to see where you went wrong and what areas you need to improve!

PERT Math Practice Test							
Practice Test 1				**Practice Test 2**			
1	A	**16**	C	**1**	C	**16**	C
2	B	**17**	D	**2**	D	**17**	D
3	C	**18**	B	**3**	A	**18**	D
4	C	**19**	D	**4**	A	**19**	B
5	D	**20**	B	**5**	C	**20**	B
6	B	**21**	A	**6**	D	**21**	D
7	C	**22**	C	**7**	D	**22**	A
8	B	**23**	A	**8**	C	**23**	C
9	B	**24**	A	**9**	B	**24**	D
10	D	**25**	C	**10**	C	**25**	B
11	C	**26**	C	**11**	A	**26**	A
12	B	**27**	A	**12**	A	**27**	A
13	A	**28**	C	**13**	B	**28**	B
14	A	**29**	C	**14**	D	**29**	B
15	D	**30**	D	**15**	A	**30**	C

PERT Practice Test 1

Answers and Explanations

1) Answer: A

Rewriting each fraction with common denominator or converting each fraction to decimal and order the decimal from least to greatest.

$\frac{3}{7} = 0.43$ $\qquad$ $\frac{5}{9} = 0.56$ $\quad$ $\frac{1}{3} = 0.33$ $\qquad$ $\frac{19}{21} = 0.9$ $\qquad$ $\frac{11}{18} = 0.61$

2) Answer: B

calculating Elena's total earnings: 35 hours × $9.20 an hour = $322

Next, divide this total by her brother's hourly rate: $322 ÷ $11.50 = 28 hours

3) Answer: C

number of fiction books: x

number of nonfiction books: $x + 1,200$

Total number of books: $x + (x + 12,000)$

40% of the total number of books are fiction, Therefore:

$40\%[x + (x + 1,200)] = x \rightarrow 0.4(2x + 1,200) = x$

$0.8x + 480 = x \rightarrow 480 = x - 0.8x \rightarrow 0.2x = 480$

$\rightarrow x = 2,400$ number of fictions

$x + 1,200 = 2,400 + 1,200 = 3,600$, the number of nonfiction books

$2,400 + 3,600 = 6,000$, the total number of books in the library

4) Answer: C

For odd index we can have negative radicand.

In the even index, negative radicand is undefined.

$\sqrt{-81}$ has a negative number under the even index, so it is non-real

Negative numbers don't have real square roots, because negative and positive integer squared is either positive or 0.

5) Answer: D

$3f(2a) = 540 \rightarrow$ (divide by 3): $f(2a) = 180$

(subtitute 2a) $5(2a)^2 = 180 \rightarrow$ (divide by 5): $(2a)^2 = 36 \rightarrow 4a^2 = 36 \rightarrow$

$a^2 = 9 \rightarrow a = 3$

6) Answer: B

Use formula to raise a number: $(x^a)^b = x^{ab}$

$3^4 = (3^2)^2 = 9^2$

7) Answer: C

Simple interest rate: I = prt (I = interest, p = principal, r = rate, t = time)

$I = 3,800 \times 0.045 \times 3 = 513$

8) Answer: B

The scale is: 5 cm:1km, (5 cm on the map represents an actual distance of 1 km).

first necessary to rewrite the scale ratio in terms of units squared:

5^2cm square:1^2km square, which gives:$25\ cm^2 : 1\ km^2$

Then, $\frac{25\ cm^2}{1km^2} = \frac{80\ cm^2}{x\ km^2}$, (where x is the unknown actual area).

Every proportion you write should maintain consistency in the ratios described

(km^2 both occupy the denominator).

Cross-multiply and isolate to solve for the unknown area x:

$x.\frac{25\ cm^2}{1km^2} = 80\ cm^2 \rightarrow x = 80\ cm^2.\frac{1\ km^2}{25\ cm^2} \rightarrow x = 3.2\ km^2$

9) Answer: B

4 more: +4

Ratio: $\div$; Ratio of a number to 5: $\frac{x}{5}$

7 less: -7 ; 7 less than the number: $x - 7$

$4 + \frac{x}{5} = x - 7$

10) Answer: D

A straight angle is an angle measured exactly $180°$

$$55° + 30° = 85°$$

$$180° - 85° = 95°$$

11) Answer: C

$$\frac{32x^5y^7z^{-2}}{12\,x^2y^9z^0} = \frac{32}{12} \times \frac{x^5}{x^2} \times \frac{y^7}{y^9} \times \frac{z^{-2}}{z^0} = \frac{8}{3} \times x^3 \times \frac{1}{y^2} \times \frac{1}{z^2} = \frac{8x^3}{3\,y^2z^2}$$

12) Answer: B

$$m = \frac{y_2 - y_1}{x_2 - x_1} = \frac{2 - (-1)}{4 - 2} = \frac{3}{2}$$

$$y - y_1 = m(x - x_1) \rightarrow y - (-1) = \frac{3}{2}(x - 2)$$

$$y + 1 = \frac{3}{2}(x - 2) \rightarrow 2(y + 1) = 3(x - 2) \rightarrow 2y + 2 = 3x - 6$$

$$2y - 3x = -6 - 2 \rightarrow 2y - 3x = -8$$

13) Answer: A

Two points are $(0,2)$ and $(6,5)$: $m = \frac{y_2 - y_1}{x_2 - x_1} = \frac{5 - 2}{6 - 0} = \frac{3}{6} = \frac{1}{2}$

$$y - y_1 = m(x - x_1) \rightarrow y - 2 = \frac{1}{2}(x - 0)$$

$$y - 2 = \frac{1}{2}x \rightarrow y = \frac{1}{2}x + 2$$

14) Answer: A

Triangle third side rule: length of the one side of a triangle is less than the sum of the lengths of the other two sides and greater than the positive difference of the lengths of the other two sides.

the third side is less than 5+8=13 and greater than 8-5=3

15) Answer: D

Using the formula for mean:

$$\text{Mean} = \frac{sum\ of\ the\ several\ given\ values}{number\ of\ value\ given} = \frac{x + (x - 3) + (x - 3)}{3} = \frac{3x - 6}{3} = \frac{3(x - 2)}{3} = x - 2$$

16) Answer: C

a value that is inversely proportional to another value: $a = \frac{k}{2b-5}$ (where k is a constant of proportionality)

substitute a and b: $15 = \frac{k}{2(7)-5} \rightarrow k = 15(9) = 135$

$a = \frac{135}{2b-5}$

17) Answer: D

$\begin{cases} 5 \times (-3x + 4y = -5) \\ 4 \times (2x - 5y = 8) \end{cases} \rightarrow \begin{cases} -15x + 20y = -25 \\ 8x - 20y = 32 \end{cases}$ →add two equations:

$-7x = 7 \rightarrow x = -1$

18) Answer: B

We can Write an equation to solve the problem.

Emma Books =Mia books +5 →Mia book = Emma – 5=b-5

Emma + Mia=17

b + b − 5 = 17 → 2b − 5 = 17 → 2b = 17 + 5 → b = 11

19) Answer: D

A line perpendicular to a line with slope m has a slope of $-\frac{1}{m}$.

So, the slope of the line perpendicular to the given line is $-\frac{1}{\frac{c}{d}} = -\frac{d}{c}$.

20) Answer: B.

For a value of x to satisfy the provided equation, it must be a solution. The equation provided should be recognized as a quadratic equation, which can be factored using many methods.

3 can be divided out of both sides: $3x^2 - 18x + 27 = 0$,

$$x^2 - 6x + 9 = 0$$

In order to further simplify this expression and solve for x, we must factor. We are looking for 2 numbers that, when multiplied together, yield +9, and when added together yield −6.

+9 factors: $\pm(1 \times 9), \pm(3 \times 3)$

$$(x - 3)(x - 3) = 0$$
$$x - 3 = 0 \rightarrow x = 3$$

So, x must equal +3. This answer can be confirmed by substituting +3 into the original equation:

$3^2 - 6(3) + 9 = 9 - 18 + 9 = 0$

21) Answer: A

subtracting 6 from both sides: $-\frac{(5x-8)}{4} \geq 2$

Multiply both sides by −4: $(5x - 8) \leq -8$

This operation clears the negative sign and the denominator of 4 from the left side. Add 8 to both sides and divide by 5 to isolate x: $5x \leq 0 \rightarrow x \leq 0$

22) Answer: C.

Recall that dividing fractions is the same as multiplying the first fraction by its reciprocal (numerator and denominator are switched).

First rewrite the expression as a multiplication problem, switching numerator with denominator in the second fraction. Then, factor and simplify, where possible:

$$\frac{(x^2+5x+6)}{(2x^2-8x+8)} \times \frac{(x^2-3x+2)}{(x^2+2x-3)} = \frac{(x+2)(x+3)}{2(x-2)^2} \times \frac{(x-2)(x-1)}{(x-1)(x+3)} = \frac{x+2}{2(x-2)} = \frac{x+2}{2x-4}$$

23) Answer: A

Use percent formula: $\text{Part} = \frac{\text{percent} \times \text{whole}}{100}$

$221 = \frac{\text{percent} \times 170}{100} \Rightarrow \frac{221}{1} = \frac{\text{percent} \times 170}{100}$, cross multiply.

$22,100 = \text{percent} \times 170$, divide both sides by 170. $\rightarrow$ percent$= 130$

24) Answer: A

Since this is subtraction of 2 fractions with different denominators, their least common denominator is: $(x-2)(3x+1)$

$$\frac{5}{(x-2)} - \frac{6}{(3x+1)} = \frac{5(3x+1)-6(x-2)}{(x-2)(3x+1)} = \frac{15x+5-6x+12}{(x-2)(3x+1)} = \frac{9x+17}{(x-2)(3x+1)}$$

25) Answer: C

State the problem in a mathematical equation:

$$2x = 5x - 18 \to 2x - 5x = -18 \to -3x = -18 \to x = \frac{-18}{-3} = 6$$

$$5x - 18 = 5(6) - 18 = 12$$

26) Answer: C

$3h = 2p + 2$:

$p = 2 \to 3h = 2(2) + 2 = 6 \to 3h = 6 \to h = 2$

$p = 5 \to 3h = 2(5) + 2 = 12 \to 3h = 12 \to h = 4$

$p = 11 \to 3h = 2(11) + 2 = 24 \to 3h = 24 \to h = 8$

possible values of h: {2,4,8}

27) Answer: A

There are 6 digits in the repeating decimal (142857), so 1 would be the first, seventh, thirteenth digit and so on.

To find the 391st digit, divide 391 by 6.

$391 \div 6 = 65$ R1

Since the remainder is 1, that means the 391st digit is the same as the 1st digit, which is 1.

28) Answer: C

Each number is the sum of the previous and the number 2 places to the left.

Which is mean: $16 + 9 = 25$

29) Answer: C

Use the distributive property to open the parentheses and combine like terms where possible.

use FOIL method: First terms, Outside terms, Inside terms, and Last terms.

$(3y - x)(x - 2y) = (3y.x) + (3y. -2y) + (-x.x) + (-x. -2y)$

$= 3xy - 6y^2 - x^2 + 2xy = -x^2 + 5xy - 6y^2$

30) Answer: D

volume of the cube: $V = S^3$

S is Side length: $140\ cm = \frac{140}{100} = 1.4\ m$

$V = (1.4)^3 = 2.744\ m^3$

PERT Practice Test 2
Answers and Explanations

1) Answer: C

The smallest prime number is 2, and the largest even negative integer is −2.

$2 + 3(−2) = 2 − 6 = −4$.

2) Answer: D

State the problem in a mathematical sentence:

$a + 42 = 230 − 3a$

$a + 3a = 230 − 42$

$4a = 188 \rightarrow a = 47$

3) Answer: A

$4\frac{1}{21} − 5\frac{4}{7} + 2\frac{1}{3} = (4 − 5 + 2)\frac{1}{21} − \frac{12}{21} + \frac{7}{21} = 1\frac{1}{21} − \frac{5}{21} = \frac{22}{21} − \frac{5}{21} = \frac{17}{21}$

4) Answer: A

$|2x − 3| = 5 \rightarrow \begin{cases} 2x − 3 = 5 \rightarrow 2x = 8 \rightarrow x = 4 \\ 2x − 3 = −5 \rightarrow 2x = −2 \rightarrow x = −1 \end{cases}$

5) Answer: C

Multiply equation (2) by 3. Add two equations [(1) +3(2)]:

$\begin{cases} x − 3y = 1 \\ 6x + 3y = 6 \end{cases} \rightarrow 7x = 7 \rightarrow x = 1$

Substitute $x = 1$ into equation (1): $1 − 3y = 1 \rightarrow −3y = 0 \rightarrow y = 0$

6) Answer: D

$\sqrt[4]{4^{-8}} = \sqrt[4]{\frac{1}{4^8}} = \frac{\sqrt[4]{1}}{\sqrt[4]{4^8}} = \frac{1}{4^{\left(\frac{8}{4}\right)}} = \frac{1}{4^2} = 4^{-2} = \frac{1}{16}$

7) Answer: D

$3.21 \times 10^{-4} = 0.000321$

8) Answer: C

$x + 53 + 32 + 45 = 180 \rightarrow x + 130 = 180 \rightarrow x = 50$

9) Answer: B

use the Pythagorean theorem to find the value of unknown side.

$a^2 + b^2 = c^2 \rightarrow 20^2 = a^2 + 12^2 \rightarrow a^2 = 400 - 144 = 256 \rightarrow a = 16$

10) Answer: C

Use percent formula: Part $= \frac{\text{percent} \times \text{whole}}{100}$

Part$= \frac{18 \times 250}{100} = 45$

Last price: $250 + 45 = \$295$

11) Answer: A

There are no values of the variable that make the equation true.

12) Answer: A

There are 3 parts labeled "F" out of a total of 8 equal parts.

The probability of not spinning at "F" is 5 out of 8.

13) Answer: B

Point $1(x_A, y_A) = (-2, -7)$

Point $2(x_B, y_B) = (6, -1)$

Distance between two points $= \sqrt{(x_B - x_A)^2 + (y_B - y_A)^2}$

$\rightarrow d = \sqrt{\left(6 - (-2)\right)^2 + \left(-1 - (-7)\right)^2} = \sqrt{8^2 + 6^2} = \sqrt{64 + 36}$

$\rightarrow d = \sqrt{100} = 10$

14) Answer: D

$\sqrt{3x - 1} = 4 \rightarrow 3x + 1 = 16 \rightarrow 3x = 15 \rightarrow x = 5$

15) Answer: A

Get the equation into slop intercept form:

$y = mx + b$ where m is slope and b is y-intercept.

$x = 2y - 4$; Add 4 to both sides $\rightarrow x + 4 = 2y$; Dividing by 2: $\rightarrow y = \frac{1}{2}x + 2$

Thus, the y-intercept is 2.

16) Answer: C

$3^{2x} = 81 \rightarrow (3^2)^x = 81 \rightarrow 9^x = 9^2 \rightarrow x = 2$

17) Answer: D

Write the equation into standard form: $x^2 + x = 30 \rightarrow x^2 + x - 30 = 0$

Factor this expression: $(x - 5)(x + 6) = 0 \rightarrow x = 5 \; or, x = -6 \rightarrow x^2 = \begin{cases} 25 \\ 36 \end{cases}$

18) Answer: D

The minimum amount of water: $5 \times \frac{3}{5} = 3$; $3 \div 2 = 1.5$

The maximum amount of water: $5 \times \frac{3}{5} = 3$

Amount of water in all pitchers: $1.5 < w < 3$

19) Answer: B

Factor the expression: $\frac{2x^2 - 7x - 4}{4(x^2 - \frac{1}{4})} = \frac{(x-4)(2x+1)}{4x^2-1} = \frac{(x-4)(2x+1)}{(2x-1)(2x+1)} = \frac{x-4}{2x-1}$

20) Answer: B

$\frac{(5x^{-2}y^3)^2}{125y^{-2}z^{-1}} = \frac{25x^{-4}y^6}{125y^{-2}z^{-1}} = \frac{y^8z}{5x^4}$

21) Answer: D

First equation: $2y - 1 = 4x + 5 \rightarrow 2y = 4x + 6 \rightarrow y = 2x + 3 \rightarrow m_1 = 2$

Second question: $4y - 1 = 2x + 5 \rightarrow 4y = 2x + 6 \rightarrow y = \frac{1}{2}x + \frac{3}{2} \rightarrow m_2 = \frac{1}{2}$

$m_1 = 2$ and $m_2 = \frac{1}{2}$, they aren't equal slopes or negative reciprocals.

22) Answer: A

Two points are (6,6) and (−10,−2) $\rightarrow m = \frac{y_2-y_1}{x_2-x_1} = \frac{-2-6}{-10-6} = \frac{-8}{-16} = \frac{1}{2}$

23) Answer: C

f(a) = 5a − 2 and f(a) = −12: 5a − 2 = −12 so that 5a = −10 and a = −2.

f(b) = 5b − 2 and f(b) = 13: 5b − 2 = 13 so that 5b = 15 and b = 3

Finally, f(a + b) = f(−2 + 3) = f(1)

f(1) = 5(1) − 2 = 3.

24) Answer: D

$xy − 5x = 32 \rightarrow x(y − 5) = 32$

$8x = 32 \rightarrow x = 4$

25) Answer: B

The formula for measurement of each angle of a regular polygon:

$x = \frac{180(n−2)}{n}$, (x is the measurement of the interior angle; n is the number of sides)

Substituting the given information:

$\frac{180(n − 2)}{n} = 144 \rightarrow 180n − 360 = 144n \rightarrow 180n − 144\,n = 360$

$\rightarrow 36\,n = 360 \rightarrow n = 10$

The polygon has 10 angles and 10 sides.

26) Answer: A

If x is the smaller consecutive integer, then $x + 1$ is the larger consecutive

integer. Use their sum (−15) to find x:

$$x + (x + 1) = −15 \rightarrow 2x + 1 = −15 \rightarrow 2x = −16 \rightarrow x = −8$$

The two consecutive integers are −8 and −7.

One is added to the smaller integer: $−8 + 1 = −7$

and 2 is subtracted from the larger integer: $−7 − 2 = −9$

Find the product: $(−7)(−9) = 63$

27) Answer: A

$3 + (5n + 8) − (6n + 5) = 3 + 5n + 8 − 6n − 5 = 6 − n$

28) Answer: B

Two parallel lines (m & side BC) intersected by side AB

$n = 65°$ (interior angles)

29) Answer: B

Note: "@" and "#" are two "operations", and they are defined in the first two lines of the question.

Begin by evaluating $f(2)$ and $f(-1)$, Then, substitute $f(2)$ and $f(-1)$ into the first operation and substitute the appropriate values into the second operation.

$f(2) = -2(2)^2 + 3 = -8 + 3 = -5$

$f(-1) = -2(-1)^2 + 3 = -2 + 3 = 1$

$a @ b = a - 2ab$:

$\big(f(2)@ f(-1)\big) = (-5)@(1) = (-5) - 2(1)(-5) = -5 + 10 = 5$

$a\#b = 2a - b^2$:

$f(2)\#\big(f(2)@ f(-1)\big) = (-5)\#5 = 2(-5) - (5)^2 = -10 - 25 = -35$

30) Answer: C

To write a percent, move the decimal point two places to the right and follow the resulting number with the % sign. Or adding the % sign after multiplying the decimal number and 100: $0.004 \times 100 = 0.4\% = 0.40\%$

"END"

Made in the USA
Columbia, SC
21 December 2019